PIES AND TARTS

First published in France in 2012 by Marabout.
This edition published in Australia in 2013 by Murdoch Books

Murdoch Books Australia
83 Alexander Street
Crows Nest NSW 2065
Phone: +61 (0) 2 8425 0100
Fax: +61 (0) 2 9906 2218
www.murdochbooks.com.au
info@murdochbooks.com.au

Murdoch Books UK
Erico House, 6th Floor
93–99 Upper Richmond Road
Putney, London SW15 2TG
Phone: +44 (0) 20 8785 5995
Fax: +44 (0) 20 8785 5985
www.murdochbooks.co.uk
info@murdochbooks.co.uk

For Corporate Orders & Custom Publishing contact Noel Hammond,
National Business Development Manager Murdoch Books Australia

Supplies by Élodie Rambaud:
MORA: www.mora.fr

Design © Hachette Livre (Marabout) 2012
Text: © Stephane Reynaud

Publisher: Sue Hines
Translator: Melissa McMahon
Editor: Sophia Oravecz
Food Editor: Christine Osmond
Editorial Manager: Livia Caiazzo
Production Manager: Karen Small

A catalogue record for this book is available from the British Library.

Printed by 1010 Printing International Limited, China

IMPORTANT: Those who might be at risk from the effects of salmonella poisoning (the
elderly, pregnant women, young children and those suffering from immune deficiency
diseases) should consult their doctor with any concerns about eating raw eggs.

OVEN GUIDE: You may find cooking times vary depending on the oven you are using.
For fan-forced ovens, as a general rule, set the oven temperature to 20°C (35°F) lower
than indicated in the recipe.

Stéphane Reynaud

PHOTOGRAPHS
MARIE-PIERRE MOREL

PIES AND TARTS

M U R D O C H   B O O K S

Pastry power!

Where there are pies, there is inevitably pastry. Whether it is flaky, short or sweet, making pastry obviously demands special attention. It is of course better to prepare your own pie base with a good white flour, quality butter, free-range eggs ... The ingredient quantities are not divisible, but you can freeze any leftover pastry dough. You just need to put it in the refrigerator the day before you use it so it thaws out.

If you're short of time, you can also buy ready-made pastry from the shop. In that case, buy the unrolled blocks of pastry rather than ready-rolled sheets.

Other types of pastry such as filo or brik pastry, both of which can be bought ready to use, have found their place in our culinary tradition.

When you use these different pastries and roll them out, you can scatter over herbs, citrus zest, spices, dried fruit and nuts ... it gives them their own unique character.

Roll, chop, fill, glaze, decorate, bake and enjoy. Yippee!

SUCCESSFUL PÂTE BRISÉE

MAKES ABOUT 875 G (1 LB 15 OZ) OF PASTRY DOUGH
PREPARATION TIME 15 MINUTES
RESTING TIME 30 MINUTES

250 g (9 oz) cold unsalted butter

500 g (1 lb 2 oz/3⅓ cups) good-quality plain (all-purpose) flour

2 scant teaspoons salt

2 egg yolks

100 ml (3½ fl oz) ice-cold water

THE 'SABLAGE' ('RUBBING' STAGE)

Cut the butter into cubes and leave to soften slightly. Combine the flour and salt on a work surface, add the butter and work the dough with your fingertips until the mixture is 'sandy' (sablé) or resembles breadcrumbs.

BINDING THE DOUGH

Make a well in the mixture, place the egg yolks and water in the centre and mix using one hand starting from the centre of the well.

Bring the dough together into a smooth ball.

Let it rest in the refrigerator, covered with plastic wrap, for 30 minutes before using. It will keep in the refrigerator for 1 week covered in plastic wrap.

SUCCESSFUL PÂTE SABLÉE

MAKES ABOUT 1 KG (2 LB 4 OZ) OF PASTRY DOUGH
PREPARATION TIME 15 MINUTES
RESTING TIME 1 HOUR

250 g (9 oz) cold unsalted butter

400 g (14 oz/2 ⅔ cups) good-quality plain (all-purpose) flour

40 g (1½ oz) fine semolina

100 g (3½ oz) almond meal

200 g (7 oz) icing (confectioners') sugar

2 eggs

PREPARATION

Cut the butter into cubes and leave to soften slightly. Combine the flour with the semolina, almond meal and sugar on a work surface. Make a well and add the eggs, mixing with the fingertips.

Incorporate the butter, squashing it with the palm of your hand onto the work surface to get a smooth ball of dough.

RESTING

Set aside in the refrigerator for 1 hour, covered in plastic wrap, before using. This pastry dough is very crumbly and needs to be handled with care.

SUCCESSFUL PÂTE FEUILLETÉE

MAKES ABOUT 1 KG (2 LB 4 OZ) OF PASTRY DOUGH
PREPARATION TIME 1 HOUR
RESTING TIME 1 HOUR

375 g (13 oz) cold unsalted good-quality butter
500 g (1 lb 2 oz/3⅓ cups) good-quality plain
    (all-purpose) flour
2 scant teaspoons salt
250 ml (9 fl oz/1 cup) ice-cold water

PREPARATION

Flatten the butter between two sheets of plastic wrap using a rolling pin to make a square shape about 1 cm (½ inch) thick. Set aside in the refrigerator.
Combine the flour and salt on a work surface using your fingertips. Add all of the water, little by little, to make a smooth ball of dough.

INCORPORATING THE BUTTER

Roll out the dough into a cross shape, keeping the centre part slightly thicker. Use the butter as a template: each part of the cross should be roughly the size of the square of butter.
Place the square of butter in the centre. Fold each arm of the cross into the centre, making sure the edges are aligned properly.

THE 'TOURAGE' ('FOLDING–TURNING' STAGE)

To seal the butter inside the dough and create the layers, it's now time for the 'tourage': the dough is rolled and folded into three six times.
Roll the square of dough into a strip. Fold the strip into three, by folding the ends over towards the centre. Turn the dough a quarter turn and repeat. Make two fingerprints in the dough to indicate it has had two folds, wrap in plastic wrap and set aside in the refrigerator for 30 minutes.
Roll the dough out again into a strip in the opposite direction of the folding. Repeat the previous process to make two more folds of the dough. Make four fingerprints in the dough to indicate it has had four folds, wrap in plastic wrap and set aside in the refrigerator for 30 minutes.
After the resting time, complete the last two folds in the same way. The pâte feuilletée is now ready. It will keep for 3–4 days in the refrigerator covered in plastic wrap.

10

THE PIE, STEP BY STEP

1

*Roll out the puff pastry
into a large rectangle.*

THE PIE, STEP BY STEP

2

Divide the dough into two equal pieces.

Note: If there is a lot of filling, make the base of the pie larger: divide up the dough in a ratio of two-thirds to one-third.

THE PIE, STEP BY STEP

3

Place the filling on one of the two rectangles, making sure to leave a 1 cm (½ inch) border all around the edge.

THE PIE, STEP BY STEP

4

*Glaze the edges with beaten egg,
then cover with the second
rectangle of dough.*

THE PIE, STEP BY STEP

5

Seal the edges by pinching them together.

THE PIE, STEP BY STEP

6

Roll the edges inward.

THE PIE, STEP BY STEP

7

*Place the pie on a baking tray
lined with baking paper. Glaze
the whole pie with egg.*

*Note: If the pie is thick, make a 'chimney' hole
about 1 cm (½ inch) wide in the middle of the pie.
Roll up a small square of baking paper and place it inside
the chimney so that the steam can escape easily.*

THE PIE, STEP BY STEP

8

Put it in the oven,
sit tight, and enjoy!

TINS, TRIMMINGS AND DECORATION

TINS

A non-stick tin is of course the ideal for making pies—without one, any filling that has leaked out can play tricks on you when unmoulding the pie.

If you don't have a non-stick tin, you can line your pan with the baking paper you just rolled out the dough on; it will then be child's play to unmould.

A last solution is to grease and flour your pan: brush it with butter and then coat the butter with flour.

Tins with a removable base or spring-form tins (which open to release the pie easily) are also handy; a useful tool for high-quality results.

DECORATION

Decorating a pie means adding your personal touch to the dish. Pastry offcuts are perfect for this and, as a bonus, reduce waste. This is the time for sharing, when the children get involved and cover themselves in flour.

Cookie-cutters and special trimmings are also part of the pie landscape, so we'll identify the cake by decorating it with a fish, a pig, a duck ... hats off to the artist!

PIES & PASTRIES

with

VEGETABLES

or

MUSHROOMS

POTATO PIE

SERVES 6 OR MORE
PREPARATION TIME 30 MINUTES
TOTAL TOTAL COOKING TIME 45 MINUTES

Serve hot, as an entrée or main course

500 g (1 lb 2 oz) pâte brisée, or 2 packets
    shortcrust (pie) pastry
500 g (1 lb 2 oz) boiling potatoes, such as
    charlotte or Dutch cream
2 onions
150 g (5½ oz) vieux (aged) Cantal cheese
3 eggs
150 ml (5 fl oz) thin (pouring) cream
1 pinch freshly grated nutmeg
Salt and pepper

EQUIPMENT
20 cm (8 inch) spring-form cake tin

POTATO FILLING
Peel the potatoes and onions and cut them into thin slices.
Grate the Cantal cheese. For the glaze, set aside 1 egg yolk
and mix it with 3 teaspoons of cream. Combine the cream
with the remaining eggs and leftover white, add the nutmeg
and season.
Combine this mixture with the potatoes and onions.

ASSEMBLY AND COOKING
Line the cake tin with baking paper, or grease and flour it.
Roll out two-thirds of the pastry dough until 3 mm (⅛ inch)
thick and place it in the tin to cover the base and side, with
the edges hanging over the side. Fill with the potato mixture.
Glaze the edges with the egg yolk. Roll out the remaining
dough to make a second round and use it to cover the pie. Seal
the two rounds of pastry dough together by pinching the edges.
Glaze the edges with the egg mixture and roll them inward so
they stick together.
Make a pie chimney (see page 20) to let the steam out and
decorate with the pastry offcuts. Glaze the top. Place on a
pre-heated heavy-based baking tray and bake at 180°C
(350°F/Gas 4) for 45 minutes.

SILVERBEET PIE

SERVES 8 OR MORE
PREPARATION TIME 45 MINUTES, PLUS COOLING
TOTAL COOKING TIME 1 HOUR 30 MINUTES

Serve hot, as an entrée or main course

From the region of Nice

375 g (13 oz) pâte feuilletée,
    or 2 packets puff pastry
1 kg (2 lb 4 oz) silverbeet (Swiss chard)
4 small onions
4 garlic cloves
20 g (¾ oz) fresh ginger
150 ml (5 fl oz) olive oil
3 eggs
80 g (2¾ oz/¾ cup) grated parmesan cheese
80 g (2¾ oz/½ cup) pine nuts
Salt and pepper

EQUIPMENT
1.5 litre (52 fl oz/6 cup) loaf (bar) tin or terrine

SILVERBEET FILLING

Trim the silverbeet, removing the tough fibres of the stems with a vegetable peeler. Chop the green section of the leaves. Slice the white part into thin strips lengthways, then cut the strips into small 1 cm (½ inch) pieces using scissors.

Peel and finely chop the onions, garlic and ginger. In a saucepan, sauté the onions, garlic and ginger in the olive oil over medium heat until translucent. Add the silverbeet stems and cook for 5 minutes, then add the chopped leaves and cook until all the moisture has evaporated. Pour the mixture into a colander to drain and cool. It is essential to remove as much moisture as possible.

Set aside 1 egg yolk for the glaze.

Combine the grated parmesan with the remaining eggs and leftover white.

Place the pine nuts into a 200°C (400°F/Gas 6) oven for 5 minutes to lightly brown them. Combine everything with the silverbeet and season well.

ASSEMBLY AND COOKING

Line the loaf tin with baking paper, leaving the sides over-hanging, or grease and flour it. Roll out two-thirds of the pastry dough until 3 mm (⅛ inch) thick and place it in the tin to line the base and sides, with the edges hanging over the sides. Fill with the silverbeet mixture.

Glaze the edges with the egg yolk. Roll out the remaining dough to make a second rectangle and use it to cover the pie. Seal the two rectangles of pastry dough together by pinching the edges. Glaze the top. Place the tin on a pre-heated heavy-based baking tray and bake at 180°C (350°F/Gas 4) for 1 hour.

HERB AND HAZELNUT PIE

SERVES 6
PREPARATION TIME 30 MINUTES, PLUS COOLING
TOTAL COOKING TIME 3 HOURS 35 MINUTES

Serve hot, as an entrée or main course

250 g (9 oz) pâte feuilletée,
    or 1 packet puff pastry
2 eggplants (aubergine)
3 capsicums (peppers), in different colours
2 zucchini (courgettes)
4 small onions
2 sprigs rosemary
1 bay leaf
150 ml (5 fl oz) olive oil
2 bunches basil
100 g (3½ oz) hazelnuts
Salt and pepper
1 egg

VEGETABLE FILLING
Chop the eggplants, capsicums and zucchini into large cubes. Peel and finely chop the onions.
Mix the vegetables together, add 1 sprig of rosemary and the bay leaf and drizzle with the olive oil. Arrange everything in a baking dish and bake for 3 hours at 150°C (300°F/Gas 2)—they should be well stewed down. Stir the vegetables regularly during cooking.
Pluck and finely chop the basil leaves. Place the hazelnuts on a baking tray and lightly toast at 180°C (350°F/Gas 4) for 5 minutes, then rub in a clean tea towel (dish towel) to remove the skins. Add them to the slow-cooked vegetables, along with the basil leaves. Season and allow to cool.

ASSEMBLY AND COOKING
Divide the dough in half and roll out two rectangles of the same size until about 3 mm (⅛ inch) thick.
Line a baking tray with baking paper and lay one rectangle of dough on top. Spread the slow-cooked vegetables over the pastry dough, leaving a 1 cm (½ inch) border all around. Whisk the egg with 3 teaspoons of water and glaze the edges. Cover with the second piece of pastry. Seal the two rectangles of pastry dough together by pinching the edges with the back of a fork. Glaze the top of the pie and decorate with the remaining sprig of rosemary. Bake at 180°C (350°F/Gas 4) for 30 minutes.

SPINACH PIE

SERVES 6 OR MORE
PREPARATION TIME 30 MINUTES, PLUS COOLING
TOTAL COOKING TIME 40 MINUTES

Serve hot, as an entrée or main course

7 sheets filo pastry

3 onions

3 garlic cloves

150 g (5½ oz) block of parmesan cheese

100 ml (3½ fl oz) olive oil

1 kg (2 lb 4 oz) baby spinach

150 g (5½ oz) ricotta cheese

100 g (3½ oz) butter

Fine sea salt, cracked black pepper

2 teaspoons poppy seeds

EQUIPMENT

20 cm (8 inch) spring-form cake tin

SPINACH FILLING

Peel the onions and garlic and roughly chop them with a knife. Roughly chop the block of parmesan cheese.

In a large, heavy frying pan, sauté the onions and garlic in the olive oil over medium heat until translucent. Add the spinach and cook until the water has completely evaporated. It is important to remove as much moisture as possible.

Next add the parmesan and ricotta. Stew the mixture together for 10 minutes, stirring constantly. Set aside to cool.

ASSEMBLY AND COOKING

Melt the butter. Lay 1 sheet of filo pastry on the work surface, brush with the butter and season with some sea salt and cracked pepper. Cover with a second sheet of pastry at a 30° angle to the first, and butter and season in the same way. Repeat the process, using all the sheets of filo to form a rosette.

Arrange the layered filo sheets in the cake tin so the edges hang well over the side. Place the spinach–ricotta mixture in the middle and fold in the corners of each of the sheets, crumpling them at the same time.

Sprinkle with the poppy seeds and bake at 180°C (350°F/Gas 4) for 20 minutes.

PUMPKIN PIE

SERVES 6
PREPARATION TIME 35 MINUTES, PLUS COOLING
TOTAL COOKING TIME 90 MINUTES

Serve hot or cold, as an entrée

500 g (1 lb 2 oz) pâte brisée,
    or 2 packets shortcrust (pie) pastry
400 g (14 oz) jap pumpkin
2 French shallots
1½ tablespoons olive oil
1 teaspoon ground cardamom
2 tablespoons light brown sugar
100 ml (3½ fl oz) tawny port or sweet white wine
5 eggs
100 ml (3½ fl oz) thin (pouring) cream
Salt and pepper
80 ml (2½ fl oz/⅓ cup) of coffee

EQUIPMENT
20 cm (8 inch) spring-form cake tin

PUMPKIN FILLING
Cut the pumpkin in half and remove the seeds. Cut up the flesh, with the skin on, into small 1 cm (½ inch) cubes. Peel and chop the shallots. In a saucepan, gently soften the shallots in the olive oil. Add the diced pumpkin, ground cardamom, sugar and port. Cover and cook over low heat, stirring at regular intervals, for 40 minutes.
Set aside 1 egg yolk and combine with 3 teaspoons of cream. Blend the pumpkin mixture in a food processor together with the cream, remaining eggs and leftover white, season and allow to cool.

ASSEMBLY AND COOKING
Line the cake tin with baking paper, or grease and flour it. Roll out two-thirds of the pastry dough until 3 mm (⅛ inch) thick and place it in the tin, with the edges hanging over the side. Fill with the pumpkin mixture.
Brush the edges with the coffee. Roll out the remaining dough to make a second round and use it to cover the pie. Seal the two rounds of pastry dough together by pinching the edges with the back of a fork. Glaze the edges with the egg mixture and roll them inward so they stick together.
Decorate with the pastry offcuts and glaze the top of the pie. Place on a pre-heated heavy-based baking tray and bake at 180°C (350°F/Gas 4) for 45 minutes.

CARROT PIE WITH CUMIN

SERVES 6
PREPARATION TIME 35 MINUTES, PLUS COOLING
TOTAL COOKING TIME 55 MINUTES

Serve this one cold, as an entrée

500 g (1 lb 2 oz) pâte feuilletée,
   or 2 packets puff pastry
4 small yellow carrots
4 small orange carrots
4 small black carrots
4 small onions
5 eggs
200 ml (7 fl oz) thin (pouring) cream
3 teaspoons ground cumin
Salt and pepper
150 g (5½ oz) vieux (aged) Comté cheese, grated

EQUIPMENT
Round 20 cm (8 inch) cake tin

CARROT–CUMIN FILLING

Peel the carrots and cut them into 3 mm (⅛ inch) sticks. Cook the yellow and orange carrots together in boiling salted water for 10 minutes and refresh them immediately in cold water. Cook the black carrots separately in the same way, so they don't colour the others, and refresh them. Set aside.
Peel and finely chop the onions.
Set aside 1 egg yolk for the glaze. Whisk the remaining eggs and leftover white with the cream, add the cumin and season well.

ASSEMBLY AND COOKING

Line the cake tin with baking paper, or grease and flour it. Roll out two-thirds of the pastry dough until 3 mm (⅛ inch) thick and place it in the tin, with the edges hanging over the side. Fill with alternating layers: half the carrots, half the onions and half the Comté cheese. Repeat the process with the remaining ingredients and pour over the egg–cream–cumin mixture.
Glaze the edges with the egg yolk. Roll out the remaining dough to make a second round and use it to cover the pie. Seal the two rounds of pastry dough together by pinching the edges and glaze the top of the pie.
Make a light criss-cross pattern over the top with the back of a knife to decorate. Place on a pre-heated heavy-based baking tray and bake at 180°C (350°F/Gas 4) for 45 minutes.

CHANTERELLE FEUILLETÉ

SERVES 6
PREPARATION TIME 25 MINUTES, PLUS COOLING
TOTAL COOKING TIME 45 MINUTES

Serve hot, as an entrée or main course

500 g (1 lb 2 oz) pâte feuilletée,
    or 2 packets puff pastry
500 g (1 lb 2 oz) fresh chanterelle mushrooms
4 French shallots
1 bunch tarragon
60 g (2¼ oz) butter
100 ml (3½ fl oz) vermouth
200 ml (7 fl oz) + 1½ tablespoons thin
    (pouring) cream
1 teaspoon cornflour (cornstarch)
Salt and pepper
3 teaspoons fennel seeds
1 egg

CHANTERELLE MUSHROOM FILLING

Clean the mushrooms by scraping them with a knife then wiping with a damp cloth. Peel the shallots and chop them finely. Pluck the tarragon leaves.

Melt the butter in a frying pan until it colours. Add the mushrooms and sauté them over medium–high heat quickly. Add the shallots, then the vermouth, and cook until the liquid has completely evaporated. Pour in the cream, reserving the 1½ tablespoons, and allow the mixture to reduce for 5 minutes.

Blend the cornflour with the reserved cold cream, add it to the mushroom mixture and cook for another 5 minutes, stirring. Add the tarragon, season with salt and pepper and allow to cool.

ASSEMBLY AND COOKING

Divide the dough in half and roll out two rounds of the same size until about 3 mm (⅛ inch) thick.

Line a baking tray with baking paper and lay one round of dough on top. Spread the mushrooms over the pastry dough, leaving a 1 cm (½ inch) border all around. Whisk the egg and use it to glaze the edges.

Cover with the second piece of pastry. Seal the two rounds of pastry dough together by pinching the edges.

Make a pie chimney (see page 20) to let the steam out. Glaze the top and sprinkle over the fennel seeds. Bake at 180°C (350°F/Gas 4) for 30 minutes.

38

CEP MUSHROOM PIE

SERVES 6
PREPARATION TIME 25 MINUTES, PLUS COOLING
TOTAL COOKING TIME 40 MINUTES

Serve hot, as an entrée or main course

500 g (1 lb 2 oz) pâte feuilletée,
    or 2 packets puff pastry
400 g (14 oz) fresh cep mushrooms
4 garlic cloves
½ bunch of flat-leaf (Italian) parsley
50 g (1¾ oz) blanched almonds
4 slices of prosciutto
100 g (3½ oz/⅔ cup) smoked bacon, cut
    into lardons
1 egg

CEP MUSHROOM FILLING

Clean the mushrooms by scraping them with a knife then wiping with a damp cloth. Cut into 1 cm (½ inch) cubes. Peel and chop the garlic, pick and chop the parsley leaves and chop the almonds into slivers. Cut the prosciutto into thin strips.

In a non-stick frying pan over medium heat, sauté the bacon with the garlic without adding any oil, add the prosciutto, then the mushrooms and finally the almonds. Sauté everything for 5 minutes, add the parsley and allow to cool.

ASSEMBLY AND COOKING

Divide the dough in half and roll out two rectangles of the same size until about 3 mm (⅛ inch) thick.

Line a baking tray with baking paper and lay one rectangle of dough on top. Spread the mushrooms over the pastry, leaving a 1 cm (½ inch) border all around. Whisk the egg and use it to glaze the edges.

Cover with the second piece of pastry. Seal the two rectangles of pastry dough together by pinching the edges with the back of a fork. Decorate with the pastry offcuts, glaze the top of the pie and bake at 180°C (350°F/Gas 4) for 30 minutes.

MORELS EN CROÛTE

SERVES 6
PREPARATION TIME 25 MINUTES, PLUS COOLING
TOTAL COOKING TIME 45 MINUTES

Serve hot, as an entrée or main course

250 g (9 oz) pâte feuilletée,
      or 1 packet puff pastry
500 g (1 lb 2 oz) fresh morel mushrooms
      or 100 g (3½ oz) dry ones
3 small onions
50 g (1¾ oz) butter
200 ml (7 fl oz) vin jaune or fino sherry
1 teaspoon cornflour (cornstarch)
200 ml (7 fl oz) thin (pouring) cream
Salt
1 egg
1 teaspoon cracked black pepper
5 unpeeled garlic cloves

EQUIPMENT
Square 20 cm (8 inch) cake tin

MOREL MUSHROOM FILLING

Clean the fresh morels (or else soak the dried morel
mushrooms for 2 hours in hot water to rehydrate them).
Peel and chop the onions.
In a frying pan, gently sauté the onions in the butter, add the
mushrooms and the vin jaune and simmer over low heat for
15 minutes. Morels must be well cooked to eliminate any risk
of toxicity.
Blend the cornflour with the cold cream, add to the mushroom
mixture and cook for a further 5 minutes. Season with salt.
Pour the preparation into the tin and allow to cool.

ASSEMBLY AND COOKING

Roll out two-thirds of the pastry into a square slightly larger
(2 cm/¾ inch) than the cake tin. Whisk the egg and use it
to brush the edges of the tin. Cover the tin with the rolled
dough and press the edges onto the tin to make sure the
pastry sticks well.
Glaze the top of the pie with egg, sprinkle with the pepper
and arrange the garlic cloves on top.
Make small twists with the remaining dough for dipping.
Bake at 180°C (350°F/Gas 4) for 20 minutes. Break the pastry
crust and dip the pieces and the twists into the morel cream.

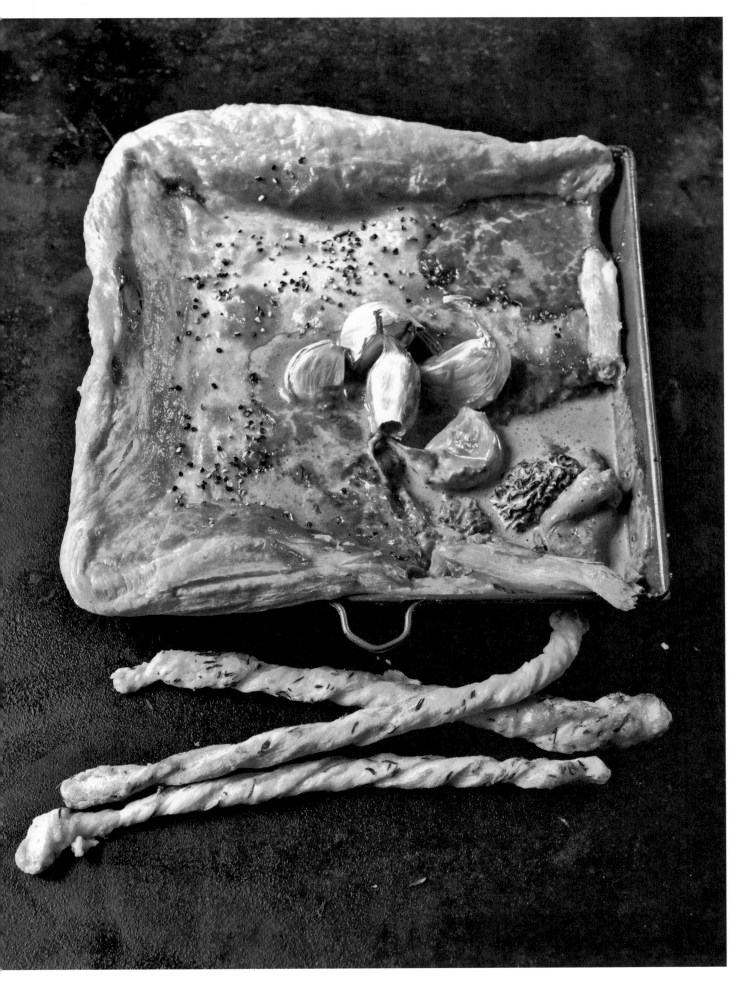

PIES & PASTRIES

with

Poultry

or

Rabbit

SUNDAY NIGHT PIE

SERVES 6
PREPARATION TIME 40 MINUTES, PLUS COOLING
TOTAL COOKING TIME 1 HOUR 5 MINUTES

Serve hot, as a main course

500 g (1 lb 2 oz) pâte brisée,
    or 2 packets shortcrust (pie) pastry
½ a cooked chicken
200 g (7 oz) cooked potatoes
200 g (7 oz) cooked carrots
3 small onions
3 garlic cloves
45 ml (1½ fl oz) olive oil
300 g (10½ oz) end-piece ham
200 g (7 oz) leftover roast veal, or other meat
3 teaspoons herbes de Provence
3 teaspoons plain (all-purpose) flour
300 ml (10½ fl oz) chicken stock
150 g (5½ oz/1½ cups) Gruyère cheese, grated
Salt and pepper
1 egg yolk

EQUIPMENT
2 litre (70 fl oz/8 cup) pie dish

MEAT FILLING

Remove the chicken from the bone and coarsely chop all of the meat and cooked vegetables. Peel and finely chop the onions and garlic.

In a frying pan, sauté the onions and garlic in the olive oil over low heat, then add the meats, herbes de Provence and flour and cook for 5 minutes. Add the vegetables and chicken stock and cook for a further 15 minutes, stirring well. Allow to cool, add the grated cheese and season.

ASSEMBLY AND COOKING

Grease and flour the pie dish. Roll out two-thirds of the pastry dough until 3 mm (⅛ inch) thick and place it in the dish, with the edges hanging over the side. Add the filling. Glaze the edges with the egg yolk.

Roll out the remaining pastry dough and cover the pie. Seal the pieces of pastry dough together by pinching the edges with the back of a fork. Decorate the top with the pastry offcuts and glaze. Place on a pre-heated heavy-based baking tray and bake at 180°C (350°F/Gas 4) for 45 minutes.

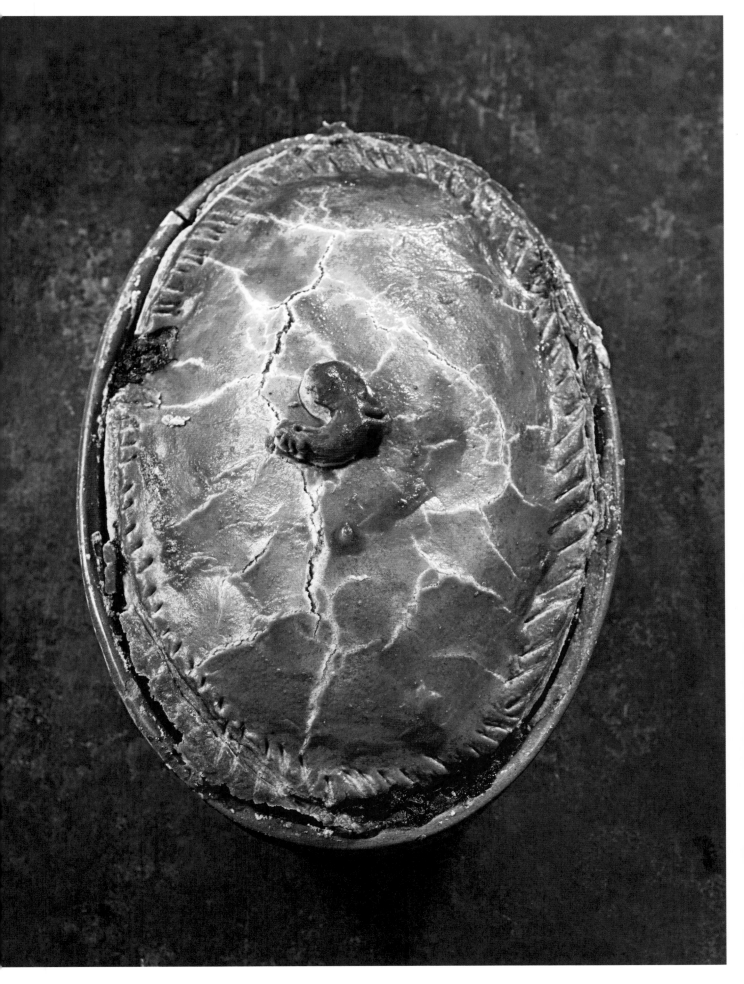

CHICKEN PIES WITH 30 CLOVES OF GARLIC

SERVES 6
PREPARATION TIME 45 MINUTES, PLUS COOLING
TOTAL COOKING TIME 2 HOURS 35 MINUTES

Serve hot, as a main course

650 g (1 lb 7 oz) pâte feuilletée,
    or 3 packets puff pastry
1 free-range chicken
4 sage leaves
2 rosemary sprigs
2 thyme sprigs
33 unpeeled garlic cloves
100 ml (3½ fl oz) olive oil
2 bay leaves
Fine sea salt and cracked black pepper
200 ml (7 fl oz) muscat wine
1 bunch basil
2 eggs

EQUIPMENT
Six 250 ml (9 fl oz/1 cup) pie tins

CHICKEN–GARLIC FILLING
Season the chicken on all sides. Chop the sage, rosemary and thyme. In a flameproof casserole dish, gently sauté 30 whole cloves of garlic in the olive oil, place the chicken on top, add the chopped herbs and bay leaves, season and moisten with the muscat. Cover with a lid and bake at 180°C (350°F/Gas 4) for 2 hours. Add a little water if necessary during cooking so the chicken doesn't stick.
Remove all the bones from the chicken—the meat should come off easily by itself. Crush the garlic cloves and remove the skin to get the pulp. Pick the basil leaves, then add the cooking juices and basil to the pulp and chicken. Coarsely chop everything with a knife and adjust the seasoning. Cool. Lightly beat the eggs. Peel and finely slice the remaining 3 garlic cloves.

ASSEMBLY AND COOKING
Grease and flour the pie tins. Roll out half the pastry dough until 3 mm (⅛ inch) thick and cut out six circles a little larger than the pie tins. Line the pie tins with the pastry, allowing the edges to hang over the sides.
Fill with the chicken–garlic mixture and glaze the edges with the eggs. Roll out the remaining pastry dough and cut out another six rounds. Cover each small pie. Seal the two rounds of pastry dough together by pinching the edges, glaze the top of the pies and scatter with slivers of garlic. Place on a pre-heated heavy-based baking tray and bake at 180°C (350°F/Gas 4) for 30 minutes.

48

CHICKEN AND TARRAGON PIE

SERVES 6
PREPARATION TIME 25 MINUTES, PLUS COOLING
TOTAL COOKING TIME 50 MINUTES

Serve hot or cold, as a main dish

400 g (14 oz) pâte feuilletée,
    or 2 packets puff pastry
3 French shallots
150 g (5½ oz) smoked duck breast
1 bunch tarragon
2 tablespoons olive oil
3 teaspoons tandoori spices
4 eggs
500 g (1 lb 2 oz) chicken breast fillet
200 ml (7 fl oz) thin (pouring) cream
Salt and pepper

TARRAGON–CHICKEN FILLING

Peel and chop the shallots. Cut the duck breast into thin slices, setting aside a few slices for decoration. Pluck the tarragon leaves.

In a saucepan, soften the shallots over low heat in the olive oil, add the duck and tandoori spices and cook for 5 minutes, stirring. Cool.

Set aside 1 egg yolk for the glaze. Process the chicken breast in a food processor with the remaining eggs and leftover white until smooth, then add the cream and season.

Using a flexible spatula, stir in the softened shallot and duck breast and add the tarragon leaves.

ASSEMBLY AND COOKING

Roll out the pastry dough into one round 5 mm (¼ inch) thick. Line a baking tray with baking paper and lay the pastry on top. Spread the chicken filling over one half of the round of pastry, leaving a 1 cm (½ inch) border from the edge.

Glaze the edges with the egg yolk and fold over the other half of the pastry round like a turnover or calzone. Seal the edges by pinching them together with the back of a fork.

Glaze the top of the pie and scatter with the slices of reserved duck breast. Bake at 180°C (350°F/Gas 4) for 45 minutes.

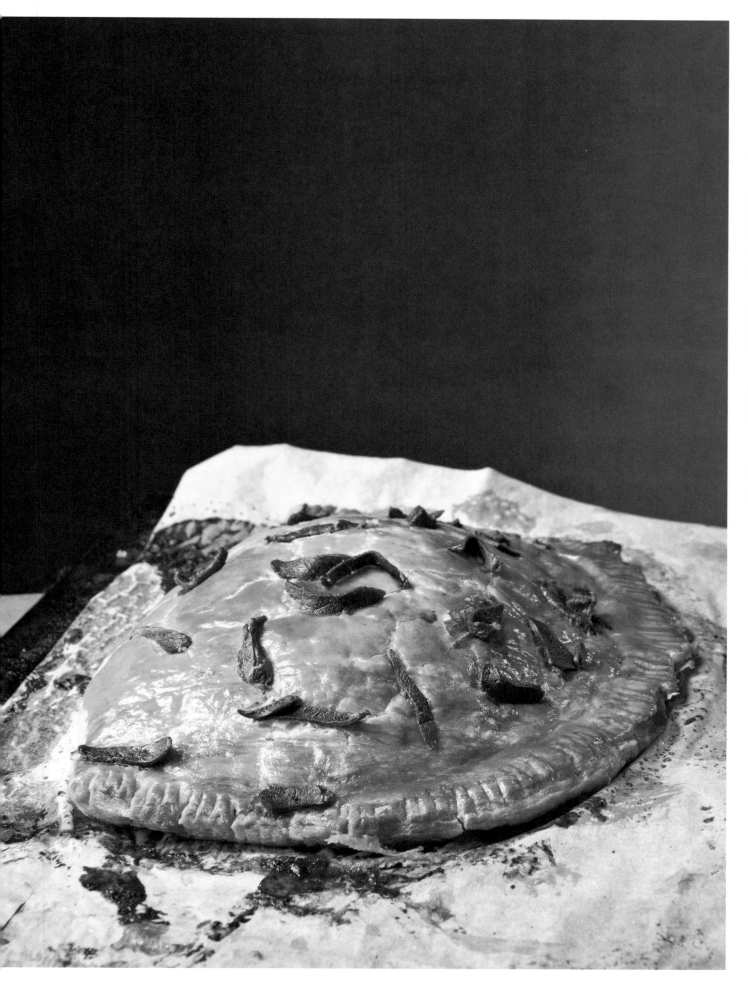

CHICKEN-CHORIZO PIE

SERVES 6
PREPARATION TIME 30 MINUTES, PLUS COOLING
TOTAL COOKING TIME 1 HOUR

Serve this one cold, as an entrée

500 g (1 lb 2 oz) pâte brisée,
    or 2 packets shortcrust (pie) pastry
3 French shallots
150 g (5½ oz) spicy chorizo
4 eggs
500 g (1 lb 2 oz) chicken breast fillet
200 ml (7 fl oz) thin (pouring) cream
2 tablespoons olive oil
100 g (3½ oz/⅔ cup) fresh shelled peas
Salt and pepper

EQUIPMENT
2 litre (70 fl oz/8 cup) pie dish

CHICKEN-CHORIZO FILLING

Peel the shallots and chop finely. Cut the chorizo into small 5 mm (¼ inch) cubes. Set aside 1 egg yolk for the glaze. Process the chicken breast in a food processor with the remaining eggs and leftover white, the cream and the olive oil until smooth. Incorporate the diced chorizo, shallots and fresh peas with a flexible spatula. Season.

ASSEMBLY AND COOKING

Grease and flour the pie dish. Roll out two-thirds of the pastry dough until 3 mm (⅛ inch) thick and place it in the dish, with the edges hanging over the side by 2 cm (¾ inch). Add the chicken–chorizo filling.
Glaze the edges with the egg yolk. Roll out the remaining dough to make a second oval and use it to cover the pie. Seal the two ovals of pastry dough together by pinching the edges, decorate with the pastry offcuts and glaze the top. Place on a pre-heated heavy-based baking tray and bake at 180°C (350°F/Gas 4) for 1 hour.

PIGEON PASTILLA

SERVES 6
PREPARATION TIME 45 MINUTES
TOTAL COOKING TIME 1 HOUR

Serve hot, as a main course

North~African inspired recipe

10 sheets brik pastry
6 small onions
50 g (1¾ oz/¼ cup) fresh ginger
4 garlic cloves
1 bunch coriander (cilantro)
1 bunch flat-leaf (Italian) parsley
6 free-range pigeons
100 ml (3½ fl oz) olive oil
Salt and pepper
3 teaspoons ground cinnamon
1 teaspoon ras el hanout spice mix
1 teaspoon freshly grated nutmeg
50 g (1¾ oz) caster (superfine) sugar
45 ml (1½ fl oz) honey
1½ tablespoons orange blossom water
200 g (7 oz/1⅓ cups) blanched almonds
6 eggs
50 g (1¾ oz) butter
30 g (1 oz/¼ cup) icing (confectioners') sugar

EQUIPMENT
20 cm (8 inch) spring-form cake tin

COOKING THE PIGEONS
Peel and chop the onions, ginger and garlic. Finely chop
the herbs.
In a flameproof casserole dish, sauté the pigeons in the olive
oil, browning them well, then season. Remove from the dish.
In the same casserole dish, cook the onions, ginger, garlic,
herbs and spices for 5 minutes, then return the pigeons to
the dish. Cover with water, cover with a lid and cook for
20 minutes.
Remove the meat and skin from the bone and chop the flesh
with a knife.

PASTILLA FILLING
Meanwhile, let the sauce reduce by half over low heat. Next,
incorporate the caster sugar, honey, orange blossom water and
coarsely chopped almonds.
Beat the eggs and add to the mixture as for scrambled eggs,
to make a thick sauce. Add the pigeon meat and adjust the
seasoning.

ASSEMBLY AND COOKING
Melt the butter and brush it over the sheets of brik pastry and
the inside of the cake tin.
Place the cake tin without its base directly onto a baking tray
lined with baking paper. Assemble the pastilla like a mille-
feuille: start with 2 sheets of brik pastry, add one-quarter
of the filling and repeat the process until you have four layers
of filling. Finish with 2 sheets of brik pastry and tuck the
edges in well.
Bake at 180°C (350°F/Gas 4) for 25 minutes. Unmould the
pastilla when you take it out of the oven. Dust with icing sugar
and, using a metal skewer heated over a flame, draw a
diamond pattern by laying the skewer on the icing sugar
several times to caramelise it.

54

DUCK CONFIT À L'ORANGE PIES

SERVES 6
PREPARATION TIME 30 MINUTES, PLUS COOLING
TOTAL COOKING TIME 40 MINUTES

Serve hot or cold, as a main dish

500 g (1 lb 2 oz) pâte brisée,
    or 2 packets shortcrust (pie) pastry
4 confit duck Marylands (leg quarters)
4 small onions
2 oranges
1 egg yolk
6 dried apricots
6 prunes
4 juniper berries
3 teaspoons duck fat
3 teaspoons light brown sugar
3 teaspoons sherry vinegar
Salt and pepper

EQUIPMENT
Six 200 ml (7 fl oz) pie tins

DUCK CONFIT À L'ORANGE FILLING
Remove the duck meat and skin from the bone, then
coarsely chop.
Peel the onions and finely chop. Juice and zest the oranges.
Combine the egg yolk with 3 teaspoons orange juice and set
aside for the glaze. Dice the apricots and prunes and crush the
juniper berries.
In a frying pan, gently sauté the onions in the duck fat until
they're lightly coloured. Add the sugar, pour in the remaining
orange juice and boil, stirring, for 30 seconds to deglaze the
pan. Reduce by half and add the vinegar, juniper berries,
dried fruit and duck. Simmer for 10 minutes over low heat.
Season and allow to cool.

ASSEMBLY AND COOKING
Grease and flour the pie tins. Roll out half the pastry dough
until 3 cm (1¼ inch) thick and cut out six circles a little larger
than the pie tins. Line the pie tins with the pastry, allowing the
edges to hang over the sides by 2 cm (¾ inch).
Fill the pie tins with the duck–orange mixture and glaze the
edges with egg. Roll out the remaining pastry dough and cut
out another six rounds. Cover each small pie. Seal the two
rounds of pastry dough together by pinching the edges, glaze
the top of the pies and scatter with orange zest. Place on a
pre-heated heavy-based baking tray and bake at 180°C
(350°F/Gas 4) for 30 minutes.

56

WILD DUCK PIE

SERVES 8 OR MORE
PREPARATION TIME 40 MINUTES
TOTAL COOKING TIME 1 HOUR 40 MINUTES

Serve this one cold, as an entrée

From the Amiens region

500 g (1 lb 2 oz) pâte feuilletée,
    or 2 packets puff pastry
4 French shallots
4 garlic cloves
100 ml (3½ fl oz) olive oil
100 ml (3½ fl oz) crème de cassis (blackcurrant
    liqueur)
1 wild duck, boned (ask your butcher)
50 g (1¾ oz) butter
45 ml (1½ fl oz) Armagnac brandy
Salt and pepper
150 g (5½ oz) speck (smoked belly pork)
200 g (7 oz) pork scotch fillet (échine de porc)
150 g (5½ oz) chicken livers
3 teaspoons juniper berries
3 rosemary sprigs
3 thyme sprigs
150 g (5½ oz) frozen blueberries
200 ml (7 fl oz) good red wine
1 egg yolk
1 teaspoon whole black peppercorns

EQUIPMENT
Mincer (grinder)
2 litre (70 fl oz/8 cup) loaf (bar) tin

DUCK FILLING

Peel and chop the shallots and garlic. In a saucepan, soften them over low heat in the olive oil, then pour in the crème de cassis and boil, stirring, for 30 seconds to deglaze the pan. Reduce until you have a syrupy consistency.

In a frying pan, fry the duck breasts in hot butter for 15 seconds on each side. Deglaze with the Armagnac, then flambé and season. Set the duck breasts aside and reserve the pan juices.

Put the rest of the duck meat with its skin, the speck and the pork through the mincer. Combine the cooking juices with the minced meat.

Remove the gall from the livers using the tip of a knife and cut the livers into 1 cm (½ inch) cubes. Combine the minced meat with the livers, crushed juniper berries, shallot syrup, chopped rosemary and thyme, blueberries and red wine. Season well.

ASSEMBLY AND COOKING

Line the loaf tin with baking paper, or grease and flour it. Roll out the puff pastry until 3 mm (⅛ inch) thick, setting aside a strip the length of the tin (and a little narrower). Place the rolled out pastry dough in the tin, with the edges hanging over the sides by 3 cm (1¼ inches).

Half fill the tin with the duck meat mixture, arrange the 2 duck breasts in the centre and cover with the remaining mixture. Fold the edges of pastry over towards the middle and glaze with the egg yolk.

Cover the pie with the strip of pastry to make a join. Glaze all over, criss-cross the joining strip with the back of a knife and sprinkle the whole peppercorns on top, pressing to make sure they stick well. Place on a pre-heated heavy-based baking tray and bake at 180°C (350°F/Gas 4) for 1½ hours.

DUCK AND FOIE GRAS PIE

SERVES 6 OR MORE
PREPARATION TIME 45 MINUTES
TOTAL COOKING TIME 1 HOUR
SETTING TIME 24 HOURS

Serve this one cold, as an entrée

500 g (1 lb 2 oz) pâte brisée,
    or 2 packets shortcrust (pie) pastry
2 duck breasts (magrets)
300 g (10½ oz) pork fillet
200 g (7 oz) fresh foie gras
80 g (2¾ oz) lardo di Colonnata, or bacon fat
200 g (7 oz) pork jowl or cheek
2 onions
1 bunch flat-leaf (Italian) parsley
200 ml (7 fl oz) sauternes wine
45 ml (1½ fl oz) Cognac brandy
1 Espelette chilli pepper
Salt
1 egg yolk
300 ml (10½ fl oz) liquid aspic, or enough
    powdered gelatine to set 300 ml (10½ fl oz)
    beef or chicken stock

EQUIPMENT
Mincer (grinder)
1.5 litre (52 fl oz/6 cup) loaf (bar) tin

DUCK AND FOIE GRAS FILLING
Cut the duck breasts, half the pork fillet, the foie gras and lardo into 1 cm (½ inch) cubes. Mince the pork jowl and the rest of the pork fillet. Peel and chop the onions, then chop the parsley. Combine all of the meats with the onions, wine, brandy, parsley and Espelette pepper. Season with salt.

ASSEMBLY AND COOKING
Line the loaf tin with baking paper, or grease and flour it. Roll out two-thirds of the pastry dough until 3 mm (⅛ inch) thick and place it in the tin, with the edges hanging over the sides. Add the filling.
Glaze the edges with the egg yolk. Roll out the remaining dough to make a second rectangle and use it to cover the pie. Seal the two rectangles of pastry dough together by pinching the edges, glaze with the egg and roll inward so they are well stuck together.
Make a pie chimney (see page 20) to let the steam out and glaze the top of the pie. Place on a pre-heated heavy-based baking tray and bake at 150°C (300°F/Gas 2) for 1 hour. Allow to cool, then, using a funnel, fill the pie with the aspic via the chimney. Allow to cool for 24 hours before serving.

60

RABBIT AND LEEK PIE

SERVES 6
PREPARATION TIME 45 MINUTES, PLUS COOLING
TOTAL COOKING TIME 2 HOURS 10 MINUTES

Serve hot, as a main course

500 g (1 lb 2 oz) pâte feuilletée,
    or 2 packets puff pastry
1 large rabbit cut into pieces
    by the butcher, liver reserved
150 g (5½ oz) spicy chorizo
4 small onions
6 garlic cloves
3 leeks
50 g (1¾ oz) butter
100 ml (3½ fl oz) olive oil
1 bay leaf
750 ml (26 fl oz/3 cups) sauvignon blanc-style
    wine
Salt and pepper
2 egg yolks

RABBIT FILLING

Cut the rabbit liver and the chorizo into 1 cm (½ inch) cubes. Peel the onions and garlic and finely chop. Wash the leeks thoroughly and slice them.

In a flameproof casserole dish, gently sauté the onions and garlic in a mixture of the butter and olive oil. Add the chorizo, the rabbit and its liver and brown.

Add the leeks and bay leaf, pour in the white wine and season. Cover and cook over low heat for 1½ hours, stirring at regular intervals.

Remove the rabbit pieces and bone them—the meat should fall off the bone by itself. Shred the meat with a fork and combine with the vegetables in the casserole dish, making sure you remove the bay leaf. Adjust the seasoning, then set aside to cool.

ASSEMBLY AND COOKING

Set aside one-quarter of the pastry dough for decoration. Divide the remaining dough in half and roll out two rectangles of the same size until about 3 mm (⅛ inch) thick.

Line a baking tray with baking paper and lay one rectangle of dough on top. Spread the rabbit mixture over the pastry, leaving a 1 cm (½ inch) border all around.

Glaze the edges with 1 egg yolk. Cover with the second piece of pastry. Seal the two rectangles of pastry dough together by pinching the edges and glaze the top.

Make thin strips from the reserved pastry dough. Make a lattice by interlacing the strips and glaze again with the remaining egg yolk. Bake at 180°C (350°F/Gas 4) for 30 minutes.

RABBIT PIES

SERVES 6 OR MORE
PREPARATION TIME 40 MINUTES
TOTAL COOKING TIME 45 MINUTES

Serve hot or cold, as an entrée or main course

500 g (1 lb 2 oz) pâte sablée,
    or 2 packets sweet rich shortcrust pastry
3 small onions
50 g (1¾ oz/¼ cup) fresh ginger
600 g rabbit meat (about 5 large thighs)
1 bunch chives
3 eggs
200 ml (7 fl oz) thin (pouring) cream
3 teaspoons honey
1 teaspoon ground cinnamon
Salt and pepper

EQUIPMENT
Mincer (grinder)
Six 8 × 5.5 cm (3¼ × 2¼ inch) loaf (bar) tins

RABBIT FILLING
Peel the onions and ginger and finely chop. Cut half the rabbit meat into small 5 mm (¼ inch) cubes and put the rest through the mincer. Finely chop the chives.
Set aside 1 egg yolk for glazing. Whisk the remaining eggs and leftover white with the cream, honey and cinnamon. Combine all the ingredients together, then season.

ASSEMBLY AND COOKING
Line the loaf tins with baking paper, or grease and flour them. Roll out two-thirds of the pastry dough until 3 mm (⅛ inch) thick and place it in the tins, with the edges hanging over the sides by 2 cm (¾ inch). Fill with the rabbit mixture.
Glaze the edges with the egg yolk. Roll out the remaining dough to make smaller rectangles and use them to cover the pies. Seal the two rectangles of pastry dough together by pinching the edges.
Make a pie chimney (see page 20) to let the steam out, decorate with the pastry offcuts and glaze. Place on a pre-heated heavy-based baking tray and bake at 180°C (350°F/ Gas 4) for 45 minutes.

RABBIT PIE WITH BASIL

SERVES 6
PREPARATION TIME 25 MINUTES
TOTAL COOKING TIME 45 MINUTES
MARINATING TIME 24 HOURS

Serve hot, as a main course

Poitevine-style

500 g (1 lb 2 oz) pâte feuilletée,
    or 2 packets puff pastry
1 rabbit, boned by the butcher
2 celery stalks with leaves
3 French shallots
150 g (5½ oz) speck (smoked belly pork)
300 ml (10½ fl oz) sauvignon blanc-style wine
45 ml (1½ fl oz) pastis (anise-flavoured liqueur)
1½ tablespoons light brown sugar
Salt and pepper
1 bunch basil
1 egg
3 teaspoons fennel seeds

MARINATING THE RABBIT

Cut the rabbit into 1 cm (½ inch) cubes. Finely chop the celery stalks with their leaves. Peel and chop the shallots. Cut the speck into thin matchsticks.
Combine the rabbit with the white wine, pastis, speck, shallots, celery and sugar. Season, cover with plastic wrap and set aside in the refrigerator for 24 hours.
Drain the mixture, pluck the leaves from the basil and chop them, then combine with the rabbit.

ASSEMBLY AND COOKING

Divide the dough in half and roll out two rounds of the same size until about 3 mm (⅛ inch) thick.
Line a baking tray with baking paper and lay one round of dough on top. Spread the rabbit mixture over the pastry, leaving a 1 cm (½ inch) border all around.
Whisk the egg and use it to glaze the edges. Cover with the second piece of pastry. Seal the two rounds of pastry dough together by pinching the edges. Glaze the top of the pie and scatter with fennel seeds. Bake at 180°C (350°F/Gas 4) for 45 minutes.

CHICKEN-RABBIT PIES WITH SPINACH

SERVES 6
PREPARATION TIME 30 MINUTES, PLUS COOLING
TOTAL COOKING TIME 1½ HOURS

Serve hot, as a main course

500 g (1 lb 2 oz) pâte brisée,
    or 2 packets shortcrust (pie) pastry
4 small onions
150 g (5½ oz) mushrooms
1 bunch sorrel
150 g (5½ oz) Fourme d'Ambert blue cheese
150 g (5½ oz) bacon, cut into lardons
Olive oil
300 g (10½ oz) baby spinach
300 g (10½ oz) chicken breast fillet
300 g (10½ oz) rabbit meat (about 3 large thighs)
Salt and pepper
1 egg

EQUIPMENT
Six 8 × 5.5 cm (3¼ × 2¼ inch) loaf (bar) tins

CHICKEN-RABBIT FILLING

Peel and finely chop the onions, thinly slice the mushrooms and chop the sorrel leaves. Cut the Fourme d'Ambert into 1 cm (½ inch) cubes.

In a saucepan, gently sauté the bacon in olive oil, add the onions and mushrooms and cook them for 15 minutes until the water has completely evaporated. Add the spinach and cook for a further 10 minutes until the water has completely evaporated.

Cut the chicken and rabbit into 1 cm (½ inch) cubes, combine them with the cooked spinach, add the chopped sorrel, Fourme and season. Cool.

ASSEMBLY AND COOKING

Roll out two-thirds of the pastry dough and cut out six rectangles of dough. Place the rectangles into the loaf tins, allowing the edges to hang over the sides by 1 cm (½ inch). Fill with the chicken–rabbit mixture. Whisk the egg and use it to glaze the edges.

Roll out the remaining pastry dough and cut out another six rectangles to fit the tins. Cover each loaf with a rectangle of dough. Seal the two rectangles by pinching the edges together. Decorate each pie with the pastry offcuts and glaze with the beaten egg. Place on a pre-heated heavy-based baking tray and bake at 180°C (350°F/Gas 4) for 1 hour.

68

3

MEAT
PIES

PÂTÉ EN CROÛTE

SERVES 6
PREPARATION TIME 30 MINUTES
TOTAL COOKING TIME 1 HOUR 30 MINUTES
MARINATING TIME 24 HOURS
SETTING TIME 24 HOURS

Serve this one cold, as an entrée

400 g (14 oz) pâte brisée,
    or 2 packets shortcrust (pie) pastry
100 g (3½ oz) chicken livers
300 g (10½ oz) veal shoulder
300 g (10½ oz) pork scotch fillet (échine de porc)
100 g (3½ oz) speck (smoked belly pork)
2 French shallots
3 garlic cloves
2 rosemary sprigs
2 thyme sprigs
1 teaspoon quatre-épices spice mix
1 bay leaf
150 ml (5 fl oz) ruby or tawny port
45 ml (1½ fl oz) Cognac brandy
Salt and pepper
300 ml (10½ fl oz) liquid aspic, or enough
    powdered gelatine to set 300 ml (10½ fl oz)
    beef or chicken stock

EQUIPMENT
Mincer (grinder)
1.25 litre (44 fl oz/5 cup) dish

MARINADE AND FILLING
The day before, clean the livers if necessary and remove the gall using the tip of a knife. Cut half the veal and pork meat, the chicken livers and the speck into small 5 mm (¼ inch) cubes.

Peel and finely chop the shallots and garlic, pluck and chop the rosemary and thyme leaves, combine with the cubed meat, add the quatre-épices and bay leaf. Moisten with the port and brandy. Cover with plastic wrap and set aside in the refrigerator for 24 hours.

Mince the rest of the meat, combine it with the drained marinated mixture, mixing well, then season and remove the bay leaf.

ASSEMBLY AND COOKING
Line the dish with baking paper, or grease and flour it. Roll out the pastry dough until 5 mm (¼ inch) thick and place it in the dish, allowing the edges to hang over the sides by 1 cm (½ inch). Add the filling and fold the pastry inward.

Bake at 180°C (350°F/Gas 4) for 1 hour, then lower the oven to 130°C (250°F/Gas 1) and bake for a further 30 minutes. Allow to cool and top with the aspic—you may not need it all. Set aside for 24 hours in the refrigerator before serving.

THREE-MEAT PIE

SERVES 6 OR MORE
PREPARATION TIME 40 MINUTES, PLUS COOLING
TOTAL COOKING TIME 1 HOUR 30 MINUTES

Serve this one cold, as an entrée

500 g (1 lb 2 oz) pâte brisée,
    or 2 packets shortcrust (pie) pastry
4 boneless rabbit thighs
300 g (10½ oz) pork scotch fillet (échine de porc)
300 g (10½ oz) boneless veal shoulder
4 garlic cloves
4 small onions
½ bunch basil
½ bunch tarragon
½ bunch flat-leaf (Italian) parsley
150 g (5½ oz) speck (smoked belly pork)
200 ml (7 fl oz) thin (pouring) cream
45 ml (1½ fl oz) rum
3 teaspoons curry powder
Salt and pepper
1 egg yolk

EQUIPMENT
Mincer (grinder)
1.5 litre (52 fl oz/6 cup) loaf (bar) tin

MEAT FILLING
Cut the rabbit, half the pork and half the veal into 1 cm
(½ inch) cubes. Put the rest of the meats through the mincer.
Peel and chop the garlic and onions. Pluck the herb leaves
and chop coarsely.
Combine all the meats, then add the cream, rum, curry
powder, herbs, onions and garlic. Season.

ASSEMBLY AND COOKING
Line the tin with baking paper, or grease and flour it. Roll
out two-thirds of the pastry dough until 3 mm (⅛ inch) thick
and place it in the tin, with the edges hanging over the sides
by 1 cm (½ inch). Add the filling. Glaze the edges with the
egg yolk.
Roll out the remaining pastry dough into a rectangle and cover
the pie. Seal the pastry together by pinching the edges, glaze
with the egg and roll the edges inward so they stick together.
Make a pie chimney (see page 20) to let the steam out and
glaze the top. Place on a pre-heated heavy-based baking
tray and bake at 180°C (350°F/Gas 4) for 1 hour, then lower
the oven to 130°C (250°F/Gas 1) and bake for a further
30 minutes.

74

PÉZENAS PIES

SERVES 6
PREPARATION TIME 45 MINUTES, PLUS COOLING
TOTAL COOKING TIME 1 HOUR

Serve hot or cold, as an entrée

From the Languedoc-Roussillon region

500 g (1 lb 2 oz) pâte brisée,
    or 2 packets shortcrust (pie) pastry
100 g (3½ oz) raisins
45 ml (1½ fl oz) Armagnac brandy
600 g (1 lb 5 oz) boneless lamb shoulder
2 small onions
1 orange
1 lemon
1½ tablespoons duck fat
1 teaspoon ground cinnamon
1 teaspoon ground nutmeg
2 tablespoons light brown sugar
Salt and pepper
1 egg

EQUIPMENT
Mincer (grinder)
10 cm (4 inch), 9 cm (3½ inch) and
    5 cm (2 inch) cookie cutters

LAMB FILLING
Plump up the raisins in 200 ml (7 fl oz) boiling water combined with the brandy for 15 minutes. Mince the lamb shoulder. Peel the onions and finely chop. Zest and juice the orange and lemon.
In a frying pan, gently sauté the onions in the duck fat, add the lamb, spices and sugar. Cook for 10 minutes over low heat. Add the zest and juice of the orange and lemon, cook for a further 10 minutes, add the raisins and season. Allow to cool.

ASSEMBLY AND COOKING
Roll out the pastry dough until 3 mm (⅛ inch) thick and cut out six 10 cm (4 inch) rounds, six 9 cm (3½ inch) rounds and six 5 cm (2 inch) rounds using the cookie cutters.
For each pie, place 1 generous tablespoon of filling on the 9 cm (3½ inch) round, leaving a small 5 mm (¼ inch) border all around. Whisk the egg and use it to glaze the edges, then cover with a 10 cm (4 inch) round. Seal the edges by pinching them together and push the filling towards the middle so you raise the dough.
Glaze with the egg. Top with a 5 cm (2 inch) round and glaze again. Bake at 180°C (350°F/Gas 4) for 30 minutes.

EASTER PIE

SERVES 6
PREPARATION TIME 45 MINUTES
TOTAL COOKING TIME 1 HOUR 30 MINUTES
MARINATING TIME 12 HOURS

Serve hot or cold, as an entrée or main course

From the Berry region

500 g (1 lb 2 oz) pâte feuilletée,
    or 2 packets puff pastry
300 g (10½ oz) veal shoulder
300 g (10½ oz) pork scotch fillet (échine de porc)
3 small onions
100 ml (3½ fl oz) rum
200 ml (7 fl oz) sauvignon blanc-style wine
1 bay leaf
150 g (5½ oz/1 cup) smoked bacon
½ bunch flat-leaf (Italian) parsley
1 teaspoon cracked black pepper
Salt
6 eggs
1 teaspoon whole black peppercorns

EQUIPMENT
Mincer (grinder)
30 cm (12 inch) long, 1.5 litre (52 fl oz/6 cup) loaf
    (bar) tin or terrine mould

MARINATING THE VEAL AND PORK

The day before, cut the veal and pork into 2 cm (¾ inch) cubes. Peel and chop the onions. Combine the meats with the onions, rum, white wine and bay leaf.
Cover with plastic wrap and set aside in the refrigerator for 12 hours.

MEAT FILLING

Chop the smoked bacon into thin matchsticks. Pluck and chop the parsley leaves. Drain the marinated meats and put them through the mincer, saving the onions from the marinade. Combine the meats and onions with the bacon and chopped parsley. Add the cracked pepper and salt.
Cook 5 eggs in boiling water for 8 minutes, rinse under cold water, then peel them.

ASSEMBLY AND COOKING

Whisk the remaining egg. Line the loaf tin with baking paper, or grease and flour it. Roll out three-quarters of the pastry dough until 3 mm (⅛ inch) thick and place it in the tin, with the edges hanging well over the sides by 3 cm (1¼ inches). Fill to two-thirds with the meat mixture, arrange the eggs in a line down the middle, lying down on their sides, then cover with the remaining filling.
Fold the pastry edges into the middle and glaze them with the egg. Roll out the remaining pastry dough into a strip. Join the edges with the strip and glaze again with the egg. Make a criss-cross pattern on the joining strip with the tip of a knife and scatter the whole peppercorns on top, pressing to make sure they stick well. Place on a pre-heated heavy-based baking tray and bake at 180°C (350°F/Gas 4) for 1½ hours.

LORRAINE PIE

SERVES 6
PREPARATION TIME 30 MINUTES
TOTAL COOKING TIME 45 MINUTES
MARINATING TIME 12 HOURS

Serve hot, as a main course

From the Lorraine region

500 g (1 lb 2 oz) pâte feuilletée,
    or 2 packets puff pastry
4 French shallots
4 garlic cloves
250 g (9 oz) veal topside (noix de veau)
250 g (9 oz) pork scotch fillet (échine de porc)
1 bunch tarragon
1 rosemary sprig
2 thyme sprigs
200 ml (7 fl oz) Gewurztraminer wine
Salt and pepper
1 egg

MARINATING THE VEAL AND PORK

Peel the shallots and garlic, then finely chop. Cut the meat into strips about 1 cm (½ inch) wide. Pluck the tarragon, rosemary and thyme leaves.
Marinate the meats with the shallots, garlic, herbs and wine. Season, cover with plastic wrap and set aside in the refrigerator for 12 hours.

ASSEMBLY AND COOKING

Divide the dough in half and roll out two rectangles of the same size until about 3 mm (⅛ inch) thick.
Line a baking tray with baking paper and lay one rectangle of dough on top. Spread over the drained strips of meat with the shallots, garlic and herbs, leaving a 1 cm (½ inch) border all around. Whisk the egg and use it to glaze the edges.
Cover with the second piece of pastry. Seal the two rectangles of pastry dough together by pinching the edges. Glaze them and roll the edges inward so they stick together.
Criss-cross the dough lightly with the tip of a knife and glaze the top of the pie. Bake at 180°C (350°F/Gas 4) for 45 minutes.

CHAMPENOIS PIE

SERVES 6
PREPARATION TIME 45 MINUTES
TOTAL COOKING TIME 1 HOUR 30 MINUTES
MARINATING TIME 12 HOURS
SETTING TIME 12 HOURS

Serve this one cold, as an entrée

From the Champagne region

500 g (1 lb 2 oz) pâte brisée,
    or 2 packets shortcrust (pie) pastry
2 garlic cloves
4 French shallots
100 g (3½ oz) chicken livers
250 g (9 oz) pork scotch fillet (échine de porc)
200 g (7 oz) fresh pork belly
200 g (7 oz) rabbit meat (3 thighs)
500 ml (17 fl oz/2 cups) brut Champagne
100 ml (3½ fl oz) Marc de Champagne eau-de-vie
1 bay leaf
½ bunch flat-leaf (Italian) parsley
Salt and pepper
1 egg
Aspic powder for 250 ml (9 fl oz/1 cup) liquid,
    or enough powdered gelatine to set 250 ml
    (9 fl oz/1 cup) liquid

EQUIPMENT
Mincer (grinder)
1.5 litre (52 fl oz/6 cup) Charlotte tin

MARINATING

Peel and chop the garlic and shallots. Clean the livers if necessary and remove the gall using the tip of a knife. Cut the pork scotch fillet, pork belly, livers and rabbit meat into small 1 cm (½ inch) pieces. Marinate with 250 ml (9 fl oz/1 cup) champagne, the Marc de Champagne, shallots, garlic and bay leaf. Cover with plastic wrap and set aside in the refrigerator for 12 hours.

FILLING

Pluck and chop the parsley leaves. Remove half the meat from the marinade and put it through the mincer. Combine the minced meat with the remaining meat. Add the parsley and season.

ASSEMBLY AND COOKING

Line the tin with baking paper, or grease and flour it. Roll out three-quarters of the pastry dough and place it in the tin, with the edges hanging over the side by 1 cm (½ inch). Add the filling. Whisk the egg and use it to glaze the edges.
Roll out the remaining pastry dough and cover the pie. Seal the two rounds of pastry dough together by pinching the edges and rolling them inward so they stick together.
Make a pie chimney (see page 20) to let the steam out, decorate with the pastry offcuts and glaze all over. Bake at 180°C (350°F/Gas 4) for 1½ hours. Allow to cool.

THE ASPIC

Using the remaining champagne as the liquid, make the aspic according to the instructions on the packet and allow to cool. Using a funnel, fill the pie with the champagne aspic via the chimney. Set aside for 12 hours in the refrigerator before serving.

MUROISE PIE

SERVES 6
PREPARATION TIME 30 MINUTES
TOTAL COOKING TIME 40 MINUTES

Serve hot, as a main course

From the Grenoble region, in Isère

500 g (1 lb 2 oz) pâte feuilletée,
    or 2 packets puff pastry
4 small onions
200 g (7 oz) mushrooms
100 g (3½ oz) pitted green olives
2 thyme sprigs
Olive oil
200 ml (7 fl oz) Chignin-bergeron-style white wine
300 g (10½ oz) veal topside (noix de veau)
300 g (10½ oz) pork scotch fillet (échine de porc)
100 g (3½ oz) bacon, cut into lardons
Salt and pepper
1 bay leaf
1 egg yolk
1 teaspoon poppy seeds
1 teaspoon fennel seeds

EQUIPMENT
Mincer (grinder)

FILLING
Peel and chop the onions. Slice the mushrooms and olives. Pluck the thyme leaves.
In a frying pan, gently sauté the onions in olive oil, add the mushrooms and olives, moisten with the wine and allow to reduce until dry.
Put the meats through the mincer, add the mushroom and thyme mixture, then season.

ASSEMBLY AND COOKING
Divide the dough in half and roll out two rectangles of the same size until about 3 mm (⅛ inch) thick.
Line a baking tray with baking paper and lay one rectangle of dough on top. Spread the filling over the pastry, leaving a 1 cm (½ inch) border all around, and place the bay leaf on top. Glaze the edges with the egg yolk.
Cover with the second piece of pastry. Seal the two rectangles of pastry dough together by pinching the edges. Glaze them and roll the edges inward so they stick together.
Decorate with the pastry offcuts, glaze the top of the pie and scatter with the poppy and fennel seeds. Bake at 180°C (350°F/Gas 4) for 30 minutes.

HAM PITHIVIER

SERVES 6
PREPARATION TIME 30 MINUTES, PLUS COOLING
TOTAL COOKING TIME 1 HOUR

Serve hot or cold, as an entrée

From the Reims region

500 g (1 lb 2 oz) pâte feuilletée,
    or 2 packets puff pastry
2 leeks
3 French shallots
100 g (3½ oz) speck (smoked belly pork)
400 g (14 oz) Reims ham, or other cooked ham,
    thickly sliced
100 ml (3½ fl oz) olive oil
200 ml (7 fl oz) dry white wine
3 teaspoons light brown sugar
1 teaspoon fennel seeds
Salt and pepper
100 g (3½ oz) blanched almonds
1 egg

FILLING

Thinly slice the leeks and rinse thoroughly. Peel and chop the shallots. Chop the speck into thin matchsticks and roughly chop the ham with a knife.

In a heavy saucepan, sauté the leeks with the shallots in the olive oil over low heat. Add the white wine and simmer for 15 minutes until the liquid has completely evaporated. Add the sugar, ham and fennel seeds and cook for a further 10 minutes. Season.

Allow to cool. Cut the almonds in four lengthways to make small slivers and add them to the mixture.

ASSEMBLY AND COOKING

Divide the dough in half and roll out two 20 cm (8 inch) rounds and place one round on a braking tray lined with baking paper. Spread the filling over the dough, leaving a 1 cm (½ inch) border all around.

Whisk the egg and use it to glaze the edges. Cover with the second piece of pastry. Seal the two rounds of pastry dough together by pinching the edges. Glaze the top of the pie. Bake at 180°C (350°F/Gas 4) for 30 minutes.

CERVELAS SAUSAGE EN CROÛTE

SERVES 6
PREPARATION TIME 30 MINUTES
TOTAL COOKING TIME 1 HOUR

Serve hot, as an entrée

Recipe of Lyonnaise origin

500 g (1 lb 2 oz) pâte brisée,
    or 2 packets shortcrust (pie) pastry
2 cervelas Lyon sausage, or other fresh pork
    sausage
2 dry Picodon cheeses (soft-rind goat's
    milk cheese)
1 bunch basil
12 thin slices of speck (smoked belly pork)
1 egg
1 teaspoon sesame seeds
1 teaspoon cracked black pepper

CERVELAS FILLING

Cook the cervelas sausages in boiling salted water for
30 minutes. Cut in half lengthways. Cut the Picodon cheeses
into thin slices. Pluck the basil leaves.
Arrange some basil leaves on one sausage half, then layer with
half the cheese slices, cover with more basil leaves and top
with the other half of the sausage, like a sandwich. Repeat
with the second sausage and wrap each sausage in six slices
of speck.

ASSEMBLY AND COOKING

Whisk the egg. Roll out two rectangles of pastry 2 cm (¾ inch)
wider than the sausages and glaze the edges with the egg.
Place 1 sausage on each rectangle and roll up, pressing firmly
where the pastry overlaps. Close the ends by pinching them
together.
Arrange the sausage rolls on a baking tray covered with
baking paper. Glaze with the egg, make a criss-cross pattern
with the point of a knife, then sprinkle with the sesame
seeds and cracked pepper. Bake at 180°C (350°F/Gas 4)
for 30 minutes.

BEEF CHEEK PIE

SERVES 6
PREPARATION TIME 30 MINUTES, PLUS COOLING
TOTAL COOKING TIME 4½ HOURS

Serve hot or cold, as a main dish

500 g (1 lb 2 oz) pâte brisée,
     or 2 packets shortcrust (pie) pastry
800 g (1 lb 12 oz) beef cheeks
6 small onions
4 carrots
1 celery stalk
1 bouquet garni
5 eggs
150 ml (5 fl oz) good red wine
1 bunch tarragon
3 French shallots
Salt and pepper

EQUIPMENT
1.7 litre (59 fl oz) loaf (bar) tin

PREPARING THE MEAT
Place the beef cheeks in a saucepan, cover with water, bring to the boil and rinse, then repeat this process and discard the water.

BEEF CHEEK FILLING
Peel the onions and carrots and cut them into small 1 cm (½ inch) cubes. Chop the celery.
Bring a pot of salted water to the boil and add the beef cheeks, bouquet garni, carrots, onions and celery, simmering them very gently for 3 hours. By the end of the cooking time, the meat should be completely falling apart. Strain and reserve the stock for another use.
Remove the bouquet garni. Retrieve the meat and vegetables, chop them up with a knife and allow to cool. Whisk 4 eggs with the red wine, pluck the tarragon leaves, finely chop the shallots and add them to the cooled chopped mixture, combining well using your hands. Season.

ASSEMBLY AND COOKING
Line the loaf tin with baking paper, or grease and flour it. Roll out two-thirds of the pastry dough until 3 mm (⅛ inch) thick and place it in the tin, with the edges hanging well over the sides by 3 cm (1¼ inches). Add the filling.
Whisk the remaining egg and use it to glaze the edges. Roll out the remaining dough to make a second rectangle and use it to cover the pie. Seal the two rectangles of pastry dough together by pinching the edges.
Make a pie chimney (see page 20) to let the steam out, decorate with the pastry offcuts and glaze the top. Bake for 1 hour at 180°C (350°F/Gas 4).

FRIAND

SERVES 6
PREPARATION TIME 20 MINUTES
TOTAL COOKING TIME 30 MINUTES

Serve hot or cold, as an entrée

Traditional recipe from the Languedoc–Roussillon region

500 g (1 lb 2 oz) pâte feuilletée,
    or 2 packets puff pastry
4 French shallots
10 sage leaves
50 g (1¾ oz) pitted black olives
6 anchovies in oil
100 g (3½ oz) sun-dried tomatoes in oil
500 g (1 lb 2 oz) sausage meat
Salt and pepper
2 eggs
3 teaspoons thin (pouring) cream
150 g (5½ oz) Ossau-Iraty-style sheep's milk
    cheese (fromage de brebis)

FILLING
Peel the shallots and finely chop. Chop the sage, black olives, anchovies and dried tomatoes. Combine the shallots, sage, olives, anchovies and tomatoes with the sausage meat and season.

ASSEMBLY AND COOKING
Roll the puff pastry into a strip 15 cm (6 inches) wide and cut out 12 rectangles of the same size.
Divide the filling into six portions and place on six of the rectangles, leaving a 1 cm (½ inch) border all around.
Whisk the eggs with the cream and cut the cheese into small 5 mm (¼ inch) cubes. Glaze the edges with egg, cover with one rectangle of pastry and seal the edges together by pinching them. Glaze again with egg, then scatter over the cubes of cheese. Bake at 180°C (350°F/Gas 4) for 30 minutes.

ESPELETTE PEPPER PIE

SERVES 6
PREPARATION TIME 45 MINUTES, PLUS COOLING
TOTAL COOKING TIME 2 HOURS

Serve this one cold, as an entrée

500 g (1 lb 2 oz) pâte brisée,
    or 2 packets shortcrust (pie) pastry
6 garlic cloves
300 g (10½ oz) veal sweetbreads (pancreas
    or 'heart' sweetbread)
200 ml (7 fl oz) milk
2 French shallots
1½ tablespoons sultanas
45 ml (1½ fl oz) Armagnac brandy
300 g (10½ oz) pork scotch fillet (échine de porc)
200 g (7 oz) pork jowl or cheek
3 teaspoons Espelette chilli powder
2 tablespoons pistachios
2 tablespoons hazelnuts
150 ml (5 fl oz) thin (pouring) cream
Salt
1 egg

EQUIPMENT
Mincer (grinder)
1.5 litre (52 fl oz/6 cup) loaf (bar) tin

PREPARING THE SWEETBREADS

Peel the garlic and remove the sprout in the middle.
Place the sweetbreads in a saucepan, add the milk and garlic, cover with water and simmer over low heat for 30 minutes. Refresh under cold water and retrieve the garlic cloves and thinly slice.
Peel the sweetbreads using a sharp knife and cut them into 1 cm (½ inch) cubes.

ESPELETTE CHILLI FILLING

Peel and chop the shallots.
Place the sultanas in a bowl, add the brandy, cover with boiling water and let stand for 10 minutes to plump them up.
Put the pork scotch fillet and jowl through the mincer.
Combine this mixture with the sweetbreads and garlic, shallots, chilli, sultanas, nuts and cream. Season with salt.

ASSEMBLY AND COOKING

Line the loaf tin with baking paper, or grease and flour it. Roll out two-thirds of the pastry dough and place it in the tin, with the edges hanging well over the sides by 3 cm (1¼ inches). Add the filling.
Whisk the egg and use it to glaze the edges. Roll out the remaining dough to make a second rectangle and use it to cover the pie. Seal the two rectangles of pastry dough together by pinching the edges.
Make a pie chimney (see page 20) to let the steam out, decorate with the pastry offcuts and glaze the top. Place on a pre-heated heavy-based baking tray and bake at 180°C (350°F/Gas 4) for 1½ hours.

SWEETBREAD PIE

SERVES 6
PREPARATION TIME 35 MINUTES, PLUS COOLING
TOTAL COOKING TIME 1 HOUR 15 MINUTES

Serve hot, as a main course

Traditional recipe from the Jura region

500 g (1 lb 2 oz) pâte feuilletée,
    or 2 packets puff pastry
6 garlic cloves
600 g (1 lb 5 oz) veal sweetbreads (pancreas
    or 'heart' sweetbread)
300 ml (10½ fl oz) milk
1 bunch tarragon
5 French shallots
1½ tablespoons olive oil
30 g (1 oz) butter
30 g (1 oz) plain (all-purpose) flour
150 ml (5 fl oz) vin jaune or fino sherry
200 ml (7 fl oz) thin (pouring) cream
1 pinch freshly grated nutmeg
Salt and pepper
1 egg

EQUIPMENT
20 cm (8 inch) spring-form cake tin

PREPARING THE SWEETBREADS
Peel the garlic and remove the sprout in the middle.
Place the sweetbreads in a saucepan, add the milk and garlic,
cover with water and simmer over low heat for 30 minutes.
Refresh under cold water and retrieve the garlic clove.
Peel the sweetbreads using a sharp knife and cut them into
1 cm (½ inch) cubes. Crush the garlic and combine with the
sweetbreads.

FILLING
Pluck the tarragon leaves. Peel and chop the shallots, then
soften them in the olive oil.
In a saucepan, melt the butter over medium heat and add the
flour all at once, stirring constantly with a wooden spoon until
the mixture comes away from the saucepan. Add the vin jaune
and the cream and cook for 5 minutes, stirring.
To this béchamel sauce, add the sweetbreads, tarragon leaves,
nutmeg and shallots. Season, then allow to cool.

ASSEMBLY AND COOKING
Place the cake tin (without its base) directly onto a baking
tray lined with baking paper. Roll out two-thirds of the pastry
dough until 3 mm (⅛ inch) thick and place it in the tin, with
the edges hanging well over the sides by 3 cm (1¼ inches).
Add the filling.
Whisk the egg and use it to glaze the edges. Roll out the
remaining dough and use it to cover the pie. Seal the two
pieces of pastry together by pinching the edges. Glaze them
and roll the edges inward so they stick together. Decorate
with the pastry offcuts, glaze again and bake at 180°C (350°F/
Gas 4) for 30 minutes.

VEAL KIDNEY PIE

SERVES 6
PREPARATION TIME 30 MINUTES, PLUS COOLING
TOTAL COOKING TIME 45 MINUTES

Serve hot, as a main course

250 g (9 oz) pâte feuilletée,
    or 1 packet puff pastry
4 veal kidneys
200 g (7 oz) speck (smoked belly pork)
3 French shallots
50 g (1¾ oz) butter
100 ml (3½ fl oz) sunflower oil
45 ml (1½ fl oz) Cognac brandy
200 ml (7 fl oz) white or tawny port
200 ml (7 fl oz) veal stock
Salt and pepper
1 egg

EQUIPMENT
Round 20 cm (8 inch) cake tin

KIDNEY FILLING
Trim the kidneys of excess fat and remove the membrane.
Cut into large cubes. Dice the speck and peel and chop
the shallots.
In a frying pan, heat the butter until it is a nut-brown colour
(beurre noisette). Add the sunflower oil and sauté the kidneys
over high heat for 2 minutes to brown. Flambé with the brandy
then drain for 10 minutes in a colander so they lose their
blood. In the same frying pan, brown the shallots, then add
the speck and cook for 10 minutes. Pour in the port and boil,
stirring, for 30 seconds to deglaze the pan. Reduce by half,
then add the veal stock and season. Cool slightly.

ASSEMBLY AND COOKING
Place the kidneys in the cake tin and cover with the speck–
shallot sauce.
Whisk the egg and use it to brush the edges of the tin.
Roll out the pastry to a round about 4 cm larger than the tin.
Cover the dish with this round and press the sides onto the
tin. Glaze all over with the egg and bake at 180°C (350°F/
Gas 4) for 30 minutes. Break the crust and eat!

BACON-SAUSAGE ROLL

SERVES 6
PREPARATION TIME 20 MINUTES
TOTAL COOKING TIME 30 MINUTES

Serve hot or cold as an entrée

500 g (1 lb 2 oz) pâte brisée, or
    2 packets shortcrust (pie) pastry
3 French shallots
1 bunch coriander (cilantro)
1 lemon
1 teaspoon ground cumin
1 teaspoon ground cinnamon
1 teaspoon ground black pepper
500 g (1 lb 2 oz) sausage meat
Salt
1 egg
6 slices smoked bacon

FILLING
Peel and finely chop the shallots. Pluck the coriander leaves and chop them. Peel and chop the lemon zest. Combine the shallots, coriander, lemon zest, spices and sausage meat and season with salt, then divide into six balls of the same size.

ASSEMBLY AND COOKING
Divide the dough into six equal portions and roll out into rounds about 5 mm (¼ inch) thick.
Place a ball of filling on each round and close up the dough, pinching it together well in the middle to seal, and roll the ball a little to smooth it out. Whisk the egg. Glaze each ball and wrap it in 1 slice of smoked bacon.
Arrange the sausage rolls on a baking tray lined with baking paper, with the bacon join underneath. Bake at 180°C (350°F/ Gas 4) for 30 minutes .

PORK TENDERLOIN FEUILLETÉ

SERVES 6
PREPARATION TIME 30 MINUTES, PLUS COOLING
TOTAL COOKING TIME 40 MINUTES

Serve hot, as a main course

500 g (1 lb 2 oz) pâte feuilletée,
    or 2 packets puff pastry
3 small onions
300 g (10½ oz) mushrooms
1 bunch tarragon
2 pork tenderloins
50 g (1¾ oz) butter
1½ tablespoons sunflower oil
Salt and pepper
1 egg
1 teaspoon herbes de Provence

FILLING
Peel the onions and finely chop them and the mushrooms.
Pluck and chop the tarragon leaves.
Trim the tenderloins of excess fat and in a frying pan in a mixture of the butter and oil, quite hot, brown them quickly for 2 minutes over high heat. Drain the tenderloins on a rack.
In the same frying pan, gently sauté the onions, add the chopped mushrooms and tarragon and cook for about 15 minutes until the water has completely evaporated. Allow to cool and season.

ASSEMBLY AND COOKING
On a baking tray covered with baking paper, roll out half of the pastry into rectangles 2 cm (¾ inch) wider than the tenderloins.
Place one-quarter of the mushroom mixture on the pastry, place a tenderloin on top and cover with another quarter of the mushroom mixture. Repeat the same process with the remaining pastry.
Whisk the egg and use it to glaze the edges. Roll the tenderloins in the pastry, seal the edges together by pinching them and close the ends. Decorate with the pastry offcuts, glaze all over with the egg and scatter with the herbes de Provence. Bake at 180°C (350°F/Gas 4) for 20 minutes.

102

WILD BOAR AND JUNIPER PIE

SERVES 6
PREPARATION TIME 40 MINUTES, PLUS COOLING
TOTAL COOKING TIME 1 HOUR 30 MINUTES

Serve this one cold, as an entrée

Traditional recipe from Sologne

500 g (1 lb 2 oz) pâte brisée,
    or 2 packets shortcrust (pie) pastry
4 French shallots
4 garlic cloves
½ bunch tarragon
400 g (14 oz) wild boar meat
150 g (5½ oz) pork scotch fillet (échine de porc)
150 g (5½ oz) pork liver
200 g (7 oz) pork jowl or cheek
3 teaspoons juniper berries
150 ml (5 fl oz) crème de cassis (blackcurrant
    liqueur)
45 ml (1½ fl oz) Cognac brandy
4 eggs
Salt and pepper

EQUIPMENT
Mincer (grinder)
1.5 litre (52 fl oz/6 cup) loaf (bar) tin

BOAR–JUNIPER FILLING

Peel the shallots and garlic, pluck the tarragon leaves and finely chop the three together. Cut 300 g (10½ oz) of the boar meat into small cubes.

Put the rest of the meats through the mincer with the juniper berries. Combine this mixture with the diced boar, add the chopped shallot–garlic–tarragon mixture, the crème de cassis, the brandy and 3 eggs, then season. Mix together by hand for a good 5 minutes.

ASSEMBLY AND COOKING

Line the loaf tin with baking paper, or grease and flour it. Roll out two-thirds of the pastry dough and place it in the tin, with the edges hanging over the sides by 2 cm (¾ inch). Add the filling.

Whisk the remaining egg and use it to glaze the edges. Roll out the remaining dough to make a second rectangle and use it to cover the pie. Seal the two rectangles of pastry dough together by pinching the edges.

Make a pie chimney (see page 20) to let the steam out, decorate with the pastry offcuts and glaze. Place on a pre-heated heavy-based baking tray and bake at 180°C (350°F/Gas 4) for 1½ hours.

TOURTE PAYSANNE

SERVES 6
PREPARATION TIME 30 MINUTES, PLUS COOLING
TOTAL COOKING TIME 1 HOUR 40 MINUTES

Serve hot, as a main course

Traditional recipe from Auvergne

500 g (1 lb 2 oz) pâte brisée,
    or 2 packets shortcrust (pie) pastry
150 g (5½ oz) smoked bacon, cut into lardons
150 g (5½ oz) cured (unsmoked) bacon, cut
    into lardons
150 g (5½ oz) ham
600 g (1 lb 5 oz) boiling potatoes, such as kipfler
    (fingerling)
4 small onions
150 g (5½ oz) vieux (aged) Cantal cheese
1 teaspoon ground nutmeg
400 ml (14 fl oz) thin (pouring) cream
Salt and pepper
1 egg

EQUIPMENT
1.5 litre (52 fl oz/6 cup) Charlotte tin

FILLING

Sauté the bacon pieces for 5 minutes in a dry frying pan over low heat. Cut the ham into matchsticks, add to the bacon and brown for a further 2 minutes.

Peel and cut the potatoes into thin 2 mm (¹⁄₁₆ inch) slices, peel and chop the onions and grate the Cantal cheese.

Combine the nutmeg with the cream and season generously.

ASSEMBLY AND COOKING

Line the tin with baking paper. Roll out two-thirds of the pastry dough until 3 mm (⅛ inch) thick and place it in the tin, with the edges hanging over the side by 2 cm (¾ inches).

Make layers of each ingredient, alternating potatoes, onions, cheese and bacon, until you run out of ingredients. Pour over the seasoned cream.

Whisk the egg and use it to glaze the edges. Roll out the remaining dough to make a second round and use it to cover the pie. Seal the two rounds of pastry dough together by pinching the edges.

Make a pie chimney (see page 20) to let the steam out, decorate with the pastry offcuts and glaze. Bake at 180°C (350°F/Gas 4) for 1½ hours. If necessary, poke a knife or skewer through the chimney to check that the potatoes are cooked.

Allow to cool for 15 minutes before serving.

CORNISH PASTY

**SERVES 6
PREPARATION TIME 45 MINUTES, PLUS COOLING
TOTAL COOKING TIME 1 HOUR 30 MINUTES**

Serve hot, as an entrée or main course

500 g (1 lb 2 oz) pâte brisée,
    or 2 packets shortcrust (pie) pastry
2 small carrots
2 small turnips
2 small potatoes
2 small onions
1 leek
300 g (10½ oz) beef steak (bavette)
200 g (7 oz) lamb shoulder
100 g (3½ oz) speck (smoked belly pork)
50 g (1¾ oz) butter
250 ml (9 fl oz/1 cup) beef stock
3 teaspoons Worcestershire sauce
10 drops Tabasco sauce
Salt
1 egg
1 rosemary sprig
1 teaspoon cracked black pepper

EQUIPMENT
Mincer (grinder)
1.5 litre (52 fl oz/6 cup) loaf (bar) tin

FILLING
Peel the carrots, turnips and potatoes and cut them into 5 mm
(¼ inch) cubes. Peel and chop the onions. Finely chop the
leek. Cook all the vegetables together in boiling salted water
for 5 minutes and drain.
Put the beef and lamb through the mincer. Dice the speck.
In a dry frying pan, brown the speck, then add the butter with
the vegetables and the meat. Cook over low heat for 10 minutes.
Add the beef stock and reduce for a further 10 minutes. Add
the Worcestershire sauce and Tabasco. Season with salt. Allow
to cool.

ASSEMBLY AND COOKING
Line the loaf tin with baking paper, or grease and flour it.
Roll out two-thirds of the pastry dough and place it in the tin,
with the edges hanging over the sides by 2 cm (¾ inches).
Add the filling.
Whisk the egg and use it to glaze the edges. Roll out the
remaining dough and use it to cover the pie. Seal the two
rectangles of pastry dough together by pinching the edges.
Make a pie chimney (see page 20) to let the steam out. Glaze,
then sprinkle with rosemary leaves and cracked pepper. Place
on a pre-heated heavy-based baking tray and bake at 180°C
(350°F/Gas 4) for 1 hour.

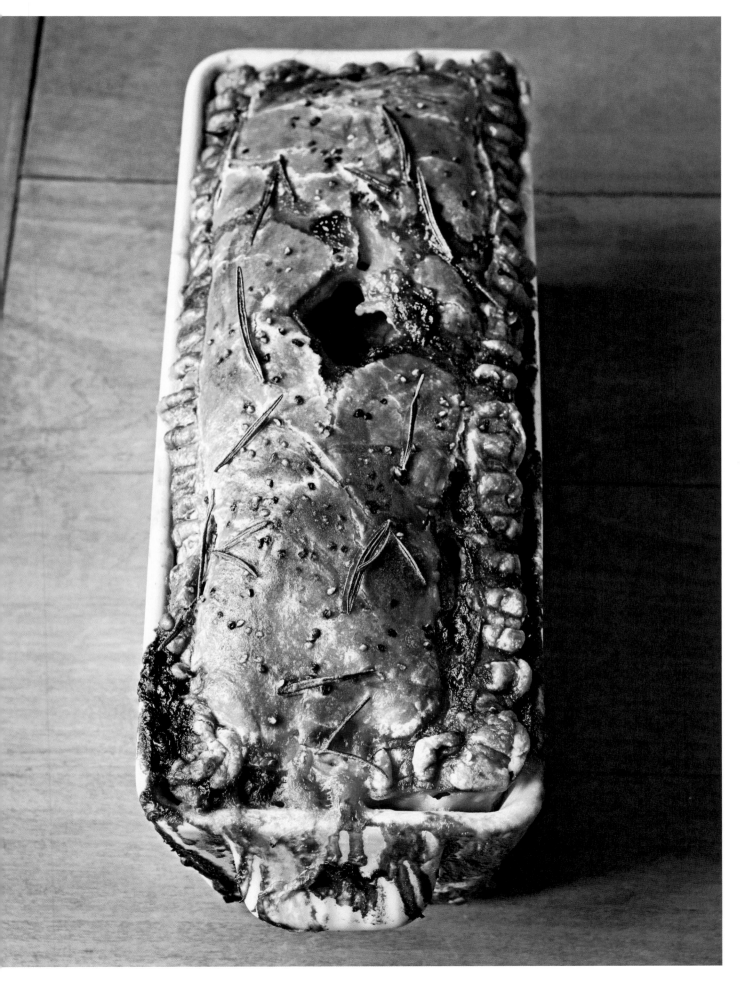

MORTEAU PIES WITH MORBIER

SERVES 6
PREPARATION TIME 45 MINUTES
TOTAL COOKING TIME 20 MINUTES

Serve hot, as a main course

Traditional recipe from the Haut-Doubs region

500 g (1 lb 2 oz) pâte brisée,
    or 2 packets shortcrust (pie) pastry
1 large saucisse de Morteau (smoked pork
    sausage)
2 French shallots
100 g (3½ oz) toasted walnuts
200 ml (7 fl oz) Arbois-style white wine
1 bunch chives
200 g (7 oz) Morbier cheese
1½ tablespoons crème fraîche
1 egg

EQUIPMENT
Six 9.5 cm (3¾ inch) pie tins

SAUSAGE FILLING

Cut the Morteau sausage into small 5 mm (¼ inch) cubes.
Peel and chop the shallots. Roughly chop the walnuts.
In a non-stick frying pan, gently sauté the Morteau sausage over low heat for 5 minutes. Add the shallots and the wine and reduce until dry.
Chop the chives and cut the Morbier cheese into 5 mm (¼ inch) cubes. Combine together and add the crème fraîche and walnuts.

ASSEMBLY AND COOKING

Grease and flour the pie tins. Roll out two-thirds of the pastry dough until 3 mm (⅛ inch) thick. Line the tins with the pastry and add the filling. Roll out the remaining dough, cut out thin strips and arrange on top of the pies like a lattice.
Whisk the egg and use it to glaze the top. Place on a pre-heated heavy-based baking tray and bake at 180°C (350°F/ Gas 4) for 20 minutes.

NÎMES PIES

SERVES 6
PREPARATION TIME 45 MINUTES, PLUS COOLING
TOTAL COOKING TIME 1 HOUR

Serve hot or cold, as an entrée

Traditional recipe from the city of the same name

500 g (1 lb 2 oz) pâte brisée, or
    2 packets shortcrust (pie) pastry
250 g (9 oz) veal shoulder
250 g (9 oz) pork scotch fillet (échine de porc)
3 garlic cloves
3 small onions
50 g (1¾ oz) dried cep mushrooms
50 g (1¾ oz/⅓ cup) pine nuts
Olive oil
150 ml (5 fl oz) thin (pouring) cream
1 teaspoon quatre-épices spice mix
Salt and pepper
1 egg yolk

EQUIPMENT
Mincer (grinder)

FILLING

Put the meats through the mincer. Peel and chop the garlic and onions. Rehydrate the mushrooms for 10 minutes in boiling water, drain, then chop coarsely. In a non-stick frying pan, toast the pine nuts over low heat for 5 minutes.
In a frying pan, gently sauté the onions with the garlic in olive oil. Add the cep mushrooms and cook for 10 minutes until the water has completely evaporated. Remove from the heat and cool. Mix together with the minced meats and add the pine nuts, cream and quatre-épices. Season.

ASSEMBLY AND COOKING

Roll out two-thirds of the pastry dough until 3 mm (⅛ inch) thick. Cut out six rounds, 15 cm (6 inches) in diameter, and place on a baking tray lined with baking paper. Divide the filling between the six rounds, leaving a 5 mm (¼ inch) border all around. Raise the edges by pinching them to give them a cylindrical form.
Roll out the remaining pastry and cut out six rounds, 8 cm (3¼ inches) in diameter. Brush the edges of the cylinder with the egg. Cover with a small 8 cm (3¼ inch) round, sealing the edges well. Glaze the tops with the egg and bake at 180°C (350°F/Gas 4) for 45 minutes.

DUCK PIE, SUD-OUEST STYLE

SERVES 6
PREPARATION TIME 40 MINUTES
TOTAL COOKING TIME 1 HOUR 30 MINUTES
MARINATING TIME 12 HOURS
SETTING TIME 24 HOURS

Serve this one cold, as an entrée

Traditional recipe from the Tauzin region

500 g (1 lb 2 oz) pâte brisée, or
    2 packets shortcrust (pie) pastry
400 g (14 oz) veal shoulder
4 small onions
750 ml (26 fl oz/3 cups) riesling wine
1 bouquet garni
4 cloves
45 ml (1½ fl oz) Cognac brandy
Salt and pepper
4 eggs
400 g (14 oz) pork scotch fillet (échine de porc)
200 g (7 oz) end-piece of ham
1 teaspoon quatre-épices spice mix
1 duck breast (magret)
Aspic powder for 400 ml (14 fl oz) liquid,
    or enough powdered gelatine to set 400 ml
    (14 fl oz) beef or chicken stock

EQUIPMENT
Mincer (grinder)
2 litre (70 fl oz/8 cup) loaf (bar) tin

MARINATING THE VEAL
The day before, cut the veal shoulder into thin 5 mm (¼ inch) slices. Peel and chop the onions. Combine the veal with 350 ml (12 fl oz) riesling, the onions, bouquet garni, cloves and brandy. Season, cover and refrigerate for 12 hours. The next day, remove the veal from the marinade, discarding the bouquet garni and the cloves.

MEAT FILLING
Set aside an egg yolk for glazing. Mince the pork and ham. Combine the onions from the marinade with the minced meat, the quatre-épices, the remaining eggs and leftover white. Trim the duck breast of fat and cut into slices 1 cm (½ inch) thick.

ASSEMBLY AND COOKING
Line the loaf tin with baking paper, or grease and flour it. Roll out two-thirds of the pastry dough until 5 mm (¼ inch) thick and line the base and sides, with the edges overhanging. Fill with alternating layers: half the minced meat mixture, half the marinated veal strips, the slices of duck in the centre, then the rest of the meat mixture and veal.
Glaze the edges with the egg yolk. Roll out the remaining dough and use it to cover the pie. Seal the pastry dough together by pinching the edges.
Make a pie chimney (see page 20) to let the steam out. Glaze the top. Place on a pre-heated heavy-based baking tray and bake at 180°C (350°F/Gas 4) for 1½ hours. Allow to cool.

THE ASPIC
Boil the remaining white wine, add the aspic powder and whisk. Allow to cool again, then fill the pie with aspic using a funnel through the chimney hole. Set aside in the refrigerator for 24 hours before serving.

114

4

PIES

with

FISH

or

SEAFOOD

TIELLE SÉTOISE

SERVES 6
PREPARATION TIME 30 MINUTES, PLUS COOLING
TOTAL COOKING TIME 1 HOUR 35 MINUTES

Serve hot, as an entrée or main course

Traditional recipe from the Languedoc–Roussillon region

500 g (1 lb 2 oz) pâte brisée,
  or 2 packets shortcrust (pie) pastry
1 kg (2 lb 4 oz) small squid
1 kg (2 lb 4 oz) tomatoes
6 garlic cloves
4 small onions
1 celery stalk
50 g (1¾ oz) pitted black olives
80 ml (2½ fl oz/⅓ cup) olive oil
150 ml (5 fl oz) dry white wine
1½ tablespoons light brown sugar
3 teaspoons paprika
Salt and pepper
1 egg yolk

PREPARING THE SQUID
Remove the tentacles from the squid, empty the inside of the tubes, cleaning them well, and rinse thoroughly. Slice the tubes into thin rings, keeping the tentacles whole.

FILLING
Remove the stems from the tomatoes, drop them into boiling water for 20 seconds and refresh them immediately under cold water. Remove the skin from the tomatoes and seed them. Roughly chop the flesh.
Peel the garlic and onions and finely chop. Slice the celery and chop the olives. In a heavy frying pan, gently sauté the squid with the celery, onion and garlic in 60 ml (2 fl oz/¼ cup) of the olive oil. Add the white wine, tomatoes, black olives and sugar. Cook over low heat for 1 hour—the mixture needs to stew together well. Allow to cool and season.
Combine the paprika with the remaining olive oil and set aside.

ASSEMBLY AND COOKING
Divide the dough in half and roll out two rounds of the same size until about 3 mm (⅛ inch) thick. Line a baking tray with baking paper and lay one round of dough on top. Spread the squid mixture over the pastry, leaving a 1 cm (½ inch) border all around.
Glaze the edges with the egg yolk. Cover with the second piece of pastry. Seal the two rounds of pastry dough together by pinching the edges, then roll them inward so they stick together.
Brush the tielle with the paprika oil and bake at 180°C (350°F/Gas 4) for 30 minutes.

KOULIBIAC

SERVES 6
PREPARATION TIME 45 MINUTES, PLUS COOLING
TOTAL COOKING TIME 1 HOUR 20 MINUTES

Serve hot, as a main course

Traditional Russian recipe

500 g (1 lb 2 oz) pâte brisée, or
    2 packets shortcrust (pie) pastry
5 eggs
4 small onions
50 g (1¾ oz) butter
150 g (5½ oz/¾ cup) uncooked basmati rice
300 ml (10½ fl oz) vegetable stock
500 g (1 lb 2 oz) fresh salmon fillet, with skin on
1 tablespoon olive oil
1 small bunch dill
150 g (5½ oz) mushrooms
1 lemon
2 tablespoons sour cream
Salt and pepper

KOULIBIAC FILLING

Cook 4 eggs for 10 minutes in boiling salted water, refresh them under cold water and remove their shells. Set them aside.

Meanwhile, peel and chop the onions. In a flameproof casserole dish, gently sauté them in the butter, add the rice and allow it to become translucent. Add the vegetable stock and cover with a sheet of baking paper with a hole in the centre. Place in a 200°C (400°F/Gas 6) oven to cook for 20 minutes, like a pilaf.

Place the salmon on a sheet of baking paper, skin side down. Brush it with olive oil and bake in the oven at 200°C (400°F/ Gas 6) for 8 minutes.

Pluck and chop the dill leaves. Chop the mushrooms. Juice the lemon and combine with the mushrooms.

Flake the salmon with a fork, combine with the rice, add the dill, then allow to cool. Incorporate the sour cream and mushrooms, then season.

ASSEMBLY AND COOKING

On a baking tray covered with baking paper, roll out one-third of the dough to make one rectangle of pastry about 3 mm (⅛ inch) thick. Spread two-thirds of the filling on top, making sure to leave a 1 cm (½ inch) border all around. Make a line of eggs lying down the centre and cover with the remaining filling.

Whisk the remaining egg and use it to glaze the edges.

Roll out the remaining pastry into a rectangle about 3 mm (⅛ inch) thick and cover the koulibiac. Seal the edges by pinching them together, decorate with the pastry offcuts and bake at 180°C (350°F/Gas 4) for 45 minutes.

Fish and seafood pies

SMOKED SALMON SPRING ROLL

SERVES 6
PREPARATION TIME 30 MINUTES
TOTAL COOKING TIME 10 MINUTES

Serve hot, as an entrée

6 sheets brik pastry
1 French shallot
1 mango
½ Lebanese (short) cucumber
150 g (5½ oz) baby spinach
150 g (5½ oz) bean sprouts
200 g (7 oz) smoked salmon
1½ tablespoons olive oil
Pepper
1 egg

SMOKED SALMON FILLING
Peel the shallot and chop finely. Peel the mango and cucumber, then cut into thin 5 mm (¼ inch) strips. Chop the spinach, trim the ends of the bean sprouts and cut the smoked salmon into thin strips.
Combine the bean sprouts, cucumber, spinach and mango. Season with the olive oil, add the shallots and season with pepper.

ASSEMBLY AND COOKING
Whisk the egg. Lay out the sheets of brik pastry.
Cover the top third of each sheet with the mango–vegetable mixture and the smoked salmon. Glaze the rest of the brik sheet with the egg.
Roll up the sheets tightly around the filling. When you've almost reached the end of the sheet, tuck in the ends and finish rolling. Brush the rolls with olive oil and bake at 200°C (400°F/Gas 6) for 10 minutes.

CROTOY PIE

SERVES 6
PREPARATION TIME 40 MINUTES, PLUS COOLING
TOTAL COOKING TIME 45 MINUTES

Serve hot, as a main course

Traditional recipe from Picardie

500 g (1 lb 2 oz) pâte brisée, or
    2 packets shortcrust (pie) pastry
4 garlic cloves
3 French shallots
45 ml (1½ fl oz) olive oil
200 ml (7 fl oz) white wine
1 kg (2 lb 4 oz) cockles, disgorged of sand
1 kg (2 lb 4 oz) green mussels, debearded
½ bunch flat-leaf (Italian) parsley
50 g (1¾ oz) butter
50 g (1¾ oz/⅓ cup) plain (all-purpose) flour
200 ml (7 fl oz) thin (pouring) cream
150 g (5½ oz) shelled cooked prawns
1 egg

EQUIPMENT
Round 20 cm (8 inch) pie tin

SHELLFISH FILLING

Peel and chop the garlic and shallots. Gently sauté them in a large frying pan in the olive oil. Add the white wine and the shellfish and allow them to open (5–7 minutes). Remove all the shellfish from their shells and set aside, reserving the cooking juices, shallots and garlic. Chop the parsley leaves.

In a saucepan, melt the butter over low heat, add the flour, stir with a wooden spoon, then blend in the cooking juices and cream. Cook for 5 minutes to thicken the sauce.

Add the chopped parsley, shellfish and prawns. Allow to cool.

ASSEMBLY AND COOKING

Grease and flour the pie tin. Roll out two-thirds of the pastry dough until 3 mm (⅛ inch) thick and place it in the tin, with the edges hanging over the side by 1 cm (½ inch). Fill with the seafood mixture.

Whisk the egg and use it to glaze the edges. Roll out the remaining dough to make a second round and use it to cover the pie. Seal the two rounds together by pinching the edges. Criss-cross the top of the pie using the tip of a knife and glaze with the egg. Place on a pre-heated heavy-based baking tray and bake at 180°C (350°F/Gas 4) for 30 minutes.

124

SALMON PIE

SERVES 6
PREPARATION TIME 30 MINUTES
TOTAL COOKING TIME 45 MINUTES

Serve hot or cold, as an entrée or main course

500 g (1 lb 2 oz) pâte feuilletée,
    or 2 packets puff pastry
800 g (1 lb 12 oz) fresh skinless salmon
1 small bunch dill
5 eggs
300 ml (10½ fl oz) thin (pouring) cream
3 teaspoons pastis (anise-flavoured liqueur)
2 French shallots
3 teaspoons fennel seeds
Salt and pepper
1 small bunch basil
1 teaspoon poppy seeds

SALMON FILLING
Cut 200 g (7 oz) of the salmon into 5 mm (¼ inch) slices.
Pluck the dill leaves. Process the rest of the salmon with the
dill, 4 eggs, the cream and the pastis in a food processor until
smooth. Finely chop the shallots. Add the fennel seeds and
chopped shallots to the salmon mixture, then season. Pluck
the basil leaves.

ASSEMBLY AND COOKING
Divide the dough in half and roll out two rectangles of the
same size until about 3 mm (⅛ inch) thick.
Line a baking tray with baking paper and lay one rectangle of
dough on top. Spread over half the salmon mixture, leaving a
1 cm (½ inch) border all around. Cover with basil leaves and
slices of salmon, then spread over the remaining mixture.
Whisk the remaining egg and use it to glaze the edges. Cover
with the second piece of pastry. Seal the two rectangles of
pastry dough together by pinching the edges. Glaze the top
of the pie and scatter with the poppy seeds. Bake at 180°C
(350°F/Gas 4) for 45 minutes.

EEL AND FENNEL PIE

**SERVES 6
PREPARATION TIME 30 MINUTES, PLUS COOLING
TOTAL COOKING TIME 50 MINUTES**

Serve this one cold, as an entrée

Traditional recipe from the Baie de Somme in Picardie

500 g (1 lb 2 oz) pâte brisée, or
    2 packets shortcrust (pie) pastry
1 red onion
3 fennel bulbs
Juice of 1 lemon
3 garlic cloves
150 g (5½ oz) peanuts
½ bunch coriander (cilantro)
300 g (10½ oz) skinless smoked eel fillets
Salt and pepper
1 egg

EEL AND FENNEL FILLING

Peel and finely chop the onion. Cook 2 bulbs of fennel in boiling salted water for 20 minutes, then drain and thinly slice. Thinly slice the remaining raw fennel bulb, juice the lemon and combine with the sliced fennel. Peel and chop the garlic, coarsely chop the peanuts, and pluck and chop the coriander leaves. In a dry frying pan, sauté the peanuts until golden. Add the garlic and cook for another minute or until lightly coloured, then add the coriander and toss to combine.

ASSEMBLY AND COOKING

Roll out one-third of the pastry into an oval about 3 mm (⅛ inch) thick and place on a baking tray lined with baking paper. Roll out the remaining pastry into an oval about 3 mm (⅛ inch) thick. Making sure to leave a 1 cm (½ inch) border all around, top the smaller oval with half of each ingredient: cooked fennel, raw fennel, onions and peanuts. Cover with the smoked eel, then top with another layer of each remaining ingredient. Season.
Whisk the egg and use it to glaze the edges. Cover with the larger oval of pastry. Seal the two ovals of pastry dough together by pinching the edges. Decorate with the pastry offcuts and glaze the top with egg. Bake at 180°C (350°F/ Gas 4) for 30 minutes.

RAINBOW TROUT AND HORSERADISH PIE

SERVES 6
PREPARATION TIME 30 MINUTES
TOTAL COOKING TIME 45 MINUTES

Serve hot or cold, as an entrée or main course

500 g (1 lb 2 oz) pâte feuilletée, or
  2 packets puff pastry
1 lemon
3 teaspoons prepared horseradish
1½ teaspoons soy sauce
800 g (1 lb 12 oz) fresh rainbow trout
3 eggs
200 ml (7 fl oz) thin (pouring) cream
1 French shallot
100 g (3½ oz/⅔ cup) fresh peas
Salt and pepper

TROUT–HORSERADISH FILLING
Combine the juice and zest of the lemon with the horseradish and soy sauce. Remove the skin and bones from the rainbow trout. Cut half the trout into 1 cm (½ inch) cubes and combine with the horseradish–lemon–soy sauce.
Process the rest of the trout in a food processor with 2 eggs and the cream. Peel and chop the shallot. In a mixing bowl, combine the processed trout with the peas, shallot and marinated trout. Season.

ASSEMBLY AND COOKING
Roll out half the pastry dough into a 3 mm (⅛ inch) thick square and place on a baking tray lined with baking paper. Spread the filling over the top, leaving a 2 cm (¾ inch) border all around.
Whisk the remaining egg and use it to glaze the edges. Roll out the remaining dough to make a second square and use it to cover the pie. Seal the two squares together by pinching the edges. Decorate with the pastry offcuts, glaze with egg and bake at 180°C (350°F/Gas 4) for 45 minutes.

130

HADDOCK AND BLACK RADISH PIE

SERVES 6
PREPARATION TIME 30 MINUTES, PLUS COOLING
TOTAL COOKING TIME 45 MINUTES

Serve this one cold, as an entrée

250 g (9 oz) pâte brisée, or
    1 packet shortcrust (pie) pastry
500 g (1 lb 2 oz) smoked haddock
2 black (or red) radishes
50 g (1¾ oz/¼ cup) fresh ginger
1 bunch chives
1 rosemary sprig
4 eggs
400 ml (14 fl oz) thin (pouring) cream
1 teaspoon Espelette chilli powder

EQUIPMENT
1 litre (35 fl oz/4 cup) loaf (bar) tin

SMOKED HADDOCK FILLING
Remove the skin and bones of the haddock and cut the flesh
into 5 mm (¼ inch) cubes. Peel and cut the radishes into 5 mm
(¼ inch) cubes. Peel and chop the ginger, chop the chives, and
pluck and chop the rosemary leaves. Whisk the eggs with the
cream and mix all the ingredients together.

ASSEMBLY AND COOKING
Line the loaf tin with baking paper, or grease and flour it.
Roll out the pastry until 5 mm (¼ inch) thick. Line the base
and sides with pastry, with the edges hanging over the side
by 1 cm (½ inch).
Pour in the haddock mixture, then place on a pre-heated
heavy-based baking tray and bake at 180°C (350°F/Gas 4)
for 45 minutes.

TUNA PIE

SERVES 6
PREPARATION TIME 30 MINUTES
TOTAL COOKING TIME 35 MINUTES

Serve hot or cold, as an entrée or main course

500 g (1 lb 2 oz) pâte feuilletée,
   or 2 packets puff pastry
3 small onions
Olive oil
100 g (3½ oz) artichokes in oil
100 g (3½ oz) sun-dried tomatoes in oil
100 g (3½ oz) of black dry-salted olives, pitted
500 g (1 lb 2 oz) canned tuna in brine
1½ tablespoons tomato sauce (ketchup)
1½ tablespoons soy sauce
1 teaspoon Tabasco sauce
1 teaspoon Worcestershire sauce
Salt and pepper
1 bunch coriander (cilantro)
1 egg

TUNA FILLING

Peel the onions, chop them finely and in a frying pan gently sauté in olive oil for 5 minutes. Dice the artichokes and dried tomatoes and coarsely chop the olives.
Drain the tuna and flake with a fork. Add the onions, olives, artichokes, tomatoes, tomato sauce, soy sauce, Tabasco and Worcestershire sauce. Adjust the seasoning. Pick and coarsely chop the coriander and add to the tuna.

ASSEMBLY AND COOKING

Divide the dough in half and roll out two rectangles of the same size until about 3 mm (⅛ inch) thick. Line a baking tray with baking paper and lay one rectangle of dough on top. Spread the tuna mixture over the pastry, leaving a 1 cm (½ inch) border all around.
Whisk the egg and use it to glaze the edges. Cover with the second piece of pastry. Seal the two rectangles of pastry dough together by pinching the edges. Decorate with the pastry offcuts and glaze the top of the pie. Bake at 180°C (350°F/Gas 4) for 30 minutes.

PRAWN AND APPLE PIE

SERVES 6
PREPARATION TIME 40 MINUTES
TOTAL COOKING TIME 1 HOUR 15 MINUTES

Serve hot, as an entrée or main course

500 g (1 lb 2 oz) pâte feuilletée, or
    2 packets puff pastry
6 tomatoes
3 small onions
1 lemongrass stem
2 tablespoons olive oil
1 teaspoon tandoori paste
60 ml (2 fl oz/¼ cup) coconut milk
1 lemon
3 granny smith apples
½ bunch coriander (cilantro)
1 chilli
18 large green prawns
Salt
1 egg

EQUIPMENT
20 cm (8 inch) spring-form cake tin

PRAWN–APPLE FILLING
Remove the stems from the tomatoes, drop them into boiling water for 30 seconds, refresh them under cold water and remove their skin and seeds. Peel and chop the onions and finely chop the lemongrass stem.

In a frying pan, gently sauté the onions in the olive oil, then add the tomato flesh, lemongrass, tandoori paste and coconut milk. Cook for 45 minutes over low heat, stirring regularly, then allow to cool.

Zest and juice the lemon. Peel the apples, cut them into 1 cm (½ inch) cubes and combine with the lemon. Chop the coriander and chilli. Peel the prawns and cut each prawn into three pieces. Combine the apples with the chopped prawns, chilli and the tomato–coconut mixture. Add the chopped coriander and season.

ASSEMBLY AND COOKING
Place the cake tin (without its base) directly onto a baking tray lined with baking paper. Roll out two-thirds of the pastry dough and place it in the tin, with the edges hanging over the side by 1 cm (½ inch). Fill with the prawn–apple mixture. Whisk the egg and use it to glaze the edges. Roll out the remaining dough to make a second round and use it to cover the pie. Seal the two rounds of pastry dough together by pinching the edges. Decorate with the pastry offcuts, glaze again with the egg, place on a pre-heated heavy-based baking tray and bake at 180°C (350°F/Gas 4) for 30 minutes.

136

SEAFOOD FEUILLETÉ FOR THE APERITIF

SERVES 6
PREPARATION TIME 25 MINUTES
TOTAL COOKING TIME 35 MINUTES

Serve hot, with drinks

As in Saint-Malo

250 g (9 oz) pâte feuilletée,
    or 1 packet puff pastry
4 garlic cloves
30 g (1 oz) fresh ginger
4 small onions
100 ml (3½ fl oz) olive oil
200 ml (7 fl oz) dry white wine
100 g (3½ oz) butter
½ bunch flat-leaf (Italian) parsley
1 chilli
1 kg (2 lb 4 oz) mussels, debearded
500 g (1 lb 2 oz) razor clams
500 g (1 lb 2 oz) clams, disgorged of sand
1 egg
1 tablespoon dill
1 teaspoon fennel seeds

EQUIPMENT
Two round 20 cm (8 inch) cake tins or pie dishes

SEAFOOD FILLING

Peel and chop the garlic, ginger and onions. In a frying pan, gently sauté them in the olive oil for 5 minutes, then add the white wine and butter and bring to the boil. Finely chop the parsley and chilli.
Clean the seafood and divide between the two cake tins. Cover with the marinière sauce and sprinkle with the chilli–parsley mixture.

ASSEMBLY AND COOKING

Roll out the pastry into two rounds about 3 mm (⅛ inch) thick with a diameter 2 cm (¾ inch) larger than the tins. Whisk the egg, brush the edges of the tins and cover with one round of puff pastry. Glaze the top of the pie, scatter with dill and the fennel seeds, then bake for 20 minutes at 180°C (350°F/ Gas 4). Break the crust and dip it in!

SMOKED HERRING PIE WITH WITLOF

SERVES 6–8
PREPARATION TIME 30 MINUTES, PLUS COOLING
TOTAL COOKING TIME 1 HOUR 15 MINUTES

Serve this one cold, as an entrée

Traditional recipe from the Nord-Pas-de-Calais region

500 g (1 lb 2 oz) pâte brisée, or
    2 packets shortcrust (pie) pastry
200 g (7 oz) witlof (chicory)
100 ml (3½ fl oz) olive oil
200 g (7 oz) kipfler (fingerling) potatoes
200 g (7 oz) carrots
250 g (9 oz) vacuum-packed smoked herring
1 red onion
1 small bunch tarragon
1 teaspoon juniper berries
2 eggs
Pepper

EQUIPMENT
1.5 litre (52 fl oz/6 cup) loaf (bar) tin

HERRING–WITLOF FILLING
Thinly slice the witlof and cook, stirring, in a frying pan in the olive oil over medium heat for 15 minutes.
Peel the potatoes and carrots and cook them for 15 minutes in boiling water (they must remain firm). Drain and cut into 5 mm (¼ inch) cubes.
Cut the herring into 5 mm (¼ inch) cubes. Peel and chop the red onion, pluck and finely chop the tarragon and crush the juniper berries. Combine all the ingredients with 1 egg, then season with pepper.

ASSEMBLY AND COOKING
Line the loaf tin with baking paper, or grease and flour it. Roll out two-thirds of the pastry dough until 3 mm (⅛ inch) thick and place it in the tin, with the edges hanging over the sides by 2 cm (¾ inch).
Whisk the remaining egg and use it to glaze the edges. Roll out the remaining dough to make a second rectangle and use it to cover the pie. Seal the two rectangles of pastry dough together by pinching the edges, decorate with the pastry offcuts and glaze the top. Place on a pre-heated heavy-based baking tray and bake at 180°C (350°F/Gas 4) for 1 hour.

140

5

CHEESE

PIES

BREBIS FINGERS

SERVES 6
PREPARATION TIME 20 MINUTES
TOTAL COOKING TIME 7–8 MINUTES

Serve hot, with drinks

Traditional recipe from the Pays Basque region

12 small sheets brik pastry
250 g (9 oz) sheep's milk cheese (fromage
de brebis), such as Ossau-Iraty
85 g (3 oz/¼ cup) black cherry jam
1 teaspoon ground sichuan pepper
1 egg

FILLING
Cut the sheep's milk cheese into 12 sticks of the same size,
1 cm (½ inch) wide and 12 cm (4½ inches) long.
Combine the black cherry jam with the sichuan pepper.
Whisk the egg.

ASSEMBLY AND COOKING
Lay out 1 sheet of brik pastry. Place 1 stick of sheep's milk
cheese at the bottom of the sheet, add 1 teaspoon of black
cherry jam and roll the pastry up tightly. Before reaching the
end, fold the sides inward, glaze the rest of the sheet with the
egg to make it stick and finish rolling. Repeat this procedure
for each sheet.
Arrange the rolls on a baking tray lined with baking paper
and bake at 200°C (400°F/Gas 6) for 7–8 minutes.

144

BRIE AND GRAPE PIES

SERVES 6
PREPARATION TIME 30 MINUTES
TOTAL COOKING TIME 30 MINUTES

Serve hot, as an entrée or the cheese course

500 g (1 lb 2 oz) pâte brisée,
    or 2 packets shortcrust (pie) pastry
150 g (5½ oz) brioche
300 g (10½ oz) raw-milk Brie de Meaux
300 g (10½ oz) white Italia grapes
3 teaspoons chestnut honey
100 g (3½ oz/⅔ cup) pistachios
1 egg

EQUIPMENT
Six 9.5 cm (3¾ inch) pie tins

BRIE AND GRAPE FILLING
Cut the brioche into small 5 mm (¼ inch) cubes and bake at 170°C (325°F/Gas 3) for about 10 minutes until they're dry and golden. Cut the Brie de Meaux into small cubes the same size as the brioche. Peel the grapes, cut them in half and remove the seeds. Combine the cubes of brioche and brie, the grapes and honey. Coarsely chop the pistachios.

ASSEMBLY AND COOKING
Grease and flour the pie tins. Cut out six rounds of pastry 2 mm (¹⁄₁₆ inch) thick to fit the tins and place the pastry rounds inside, letting them hang over the sides by 5 mm (¼ inch). Fill with the brie mixture.
Roll out the remaining pastry dough and cut out another six rounds. Whisk the egg and use it to glaze the edges, then cover each pie with one round of pastry. Glaze again and scatter over the pistachios. Place on a pre-heated heavy-based baking tray and bake at 180°C (350°F/Gas 4) for 20 minutes.

146

BLUE CHEESE AND WALNUT PIES

SERVES 6
PREPARATION TIME 20 MINUTES
TOTAL COOKING TIME 25 MINUTES

Serve hot, as an entrée or at the time of the cheese course

400 g (14 oz) pâte brisée,
    or 2 packets shortcrust (pie) pastry
100 g (3½ oz) hazelnuts
100 g (3½ oz) walnuts
100 g (3½ oz) cashews
2 tablespoons sultanas
300 g (10½ oz) Bleu d'Auvergne blue cheese
1 egg

BLUE CHEESE FILLING
Place the nuts on a baking tray and lightly toast at 180°C (350°F/Gas 4) for 5 minutes, then coarsely crush. Plump up the sultanas in boiling water for 10 minutes. Cut the blue cheese into small 5 mm (¼ inch) cubes.

ASSEMBLY AND COOKING
Divide the dough into three equal balls. Roll out three rounds about 3 mm thick. Arrange the blue cheese and three-quarters of the nuts on one half of the rounds, leaving a 1 cm (½ inch) border from the edge.
Whisk the egg and use it to glaze the edges. Fold the round over to make a turnover. Seal the edges by pinching them together, glaze the top and sprinkle the remaining nuts on top. Bake at 180°C (350°F/Gas 4) for 20 minutes.

Cheese pies

CAMEMBERT AND APPLE FEUILLETÉ

SERVES 6
PREPARATION TIME 20 MINUTES
TOTAL COOKING TIME 15 MINUTES

Serve hot, as an entrée or instead of the cheese course

250 g (9 oz) pâte feuilletée,
    or 1 packet puff pastry
3 Camemberts de Normandie, 250 g (9 oz) each
1 apple, such as reinette
45 ml (1½ fl oz) calvados
3 teaspoons cracked pepper
1 egg
2 teaspoons herbes de Provence

CAMEMBERT–APPLE FILLING

Unwrap the camemberts from their paper, then put each back in its box. Peel the apple and cut it into small 5 mm (¼ inch) sticks. Make small incisions in the camemberts with a knife and insert the sticks of apple. Pour 3 teaspoons of calvados on each of the camemberts and sprinkle with cracked the pepper.

ASSEMBLY AND COOKING

Divide the dough into three equal balls. Roll out three rounds approximately 3 cm (1¼ inches) larger than the diameter of the boxes.
Whisk the egg and use it to brush the edges of the camembert boxes. Cover with a round of pastry, sticking the edges firmly to the box.
Decorate with the pastry offcuts, glaze and sprinkle with the herbes de Provence. Bake at 180°C (350°F/Gas 4) for 15 minutes. Eat with a spoon, using the pastry like bread.

BROCCIU FEUILLETÉ

SERVES 6
PREPARATION TIME 20 MINUTES
TOTAL COOKING TIME 30 MINUTES

Serve hot, as an entrée or the cheese course

Traditional recipe from Corsica

400 g (14 oz) pâte feuilletée,
    or 2 packets puff pastry
1 lemon
4 eggs
50 g (1¾ oz) sugar
1½ tablespoons orange blossom water
300 g (10½ oz) Brocciu cheese (fresh goat
    or ewe's milk cheese)

BROCCIU FILLING
Zest the lemon.
Whisk 3 eggs with the sugar, add the orange blossom water
and lemon zest. Fold in the drained Brocciu with a spatula.

ASSEMBLY AND COOKING
Set aside one-quarter of the pastry dough for decoration.
Divide the remaining dough in half and roll out two rectangles
of the same size until about 3 mm (⅛ inch) thick. Line a
baking tray with baking paper and lay one rectangle of dough
on top. Spread the Brocciu mixture over the pastry, leaving a
1 cm (½ inch) border all around.
Whisk the remaining egg and use it to glaze the edges. Cover
with the second piece of pastry. Seal the two rectangles of
pastry dough together by pinching the edges. Glaze the top
of the pie.
Roll out the remaining dough and cut it into strips, arrange
in a lattice on the pastry, then glaze again. Bake at 180°C
(350°F/Gas 4) for 30 minutes.

PICODON IN A SWEET CRUST

SERVES 6
PREPARATION TIME 20 MINUTES, PLUS COOLING
TOTAL COOKING TIME 10 MINUTES
RESTING TIME 45 MINUTES

Serve hot, as an entrée or the cheese course

Traditional recipe from the Ardèche region

500 g (1 lb 2 oz) pâte sablée,
    or 2 packets sweet rich shortcrust pastry
2 eggs
6 Saint Agrève Picodon cheeses (soft-rind goat's
    milk cheese)
12 thin slices smoked bacon
6 rosemary sprigs

ASSEMBLY
Roll out the pastry until 3 mm (⅛ inch) thick and cut out six
rounds 1 cm (½ inch) larger than a Picodon cheese and six
rounds that are 2 cm (¾ inch) larger. Whisk the eggs.
Place 1 Picodon cheese on each smaller round and cover with
the larger round, sealing the edges by pinching them together.
Place on a baking tray lined with baking paper and glaze with
the egg.
Let them rest in the refrigerator for 45 minutes.

COOKING
Take the Picodon parcels out of the refrigerator, arrange the
slices of bacon on top in the shape of a cross, inserting 1 sprig
of rosemary between them. Bake straight away in a 200°C
(400°F/Gas 6) oven for 10 minutes.

ROUERGUE PIES

SERVES 6
PREPARATION TIME 30 MINUTES
TOTAL COOKING TIME 20 MINUTES

Serve hot, as an entrée or the cheese course

Traditional recipe from the Aveyron region

500 g (1 lb 2 oz) pâte brisée,
    or 2 packets shortcrust (pie) pastry
3 eggs
200 ml (7 fl oz) thin (pouring) cream
150 g (5½ oz) smoked bacon, cut into lardons
200 g (7 oz) Roquefort cheese
200 g (7 oz) Laguiole cheese, or other French
    semi-hard cow's milk cheese

EQUIPMENT
Six 9.5 cm (3¾ inch) pie tins

FILLING
Whisk 2 eggs with the cream. Sauté the bacon pieces for 5 minutes in a dry frying pan over low heat. Chop the Roquefort and Laguiole cheese into small 1 cm (½ inch) cubes. Combine everything together.

ASSEMBLY AND COOKING
Grease and flour the pie tins. Roll out the pastry until 3 mm (⅛ inch) thick, cut out six rounds to fit the tins and six squares that are a little smaller. Whisk the remaining egg.
Line the tins with the rounds of pastry, fill with the Roquefort mixture, cover with a square of pastry, glaze with the egg and bake at 180°C (350°F/Gas 4) for 20 minutes.

MUNSTER FEUILLETÉ

SERVES 6
PREPARATION TIME 20 MINUTES
TOTAL COOKING TIME 35 MINUTES

Serve hot or cold as an entrée

Traditional recipe from the Alsace region

500 g (1 lb 2 oz) pâte feuilletée,
    or 2 packets puff pastry
6 boiling potatoes, such as charlotte or
    Dutch cream
300 g (10½ oz) farmhouse Munster cheese
1 egg yolk
3 teaspoons cumin seeds

EQUIPMENT
Six 9.5 cm (3¾ inch) pie tins

MUNSTER CHEESE FILLING
Peel the potatoes, and cook them for about 15 minutes
in boiling water, refresh them under cold water, then slice
into rounds.
Cut the Munster cheese into thin slices and set six aside.

ASSEMBLY AND COOKING
Grease and flour the pie tins. Roll out half the pastry dough
until 3 mm (⅛ inch) thick. Cut out six rounds of pastry to fit
the tins. Line each individual tin with pastry, letting the edges
hang over the sides by 5 mm (¼ inch). Divide the potato slices
between them, then top with the cheese.
Glaze the edges with the egg yolk. Roll out the remaining
dough and cut out another six rounds. Cover each pie with one
round of pastry and seal by pressing the edges together. Glaze
all over with egg, top with a slice of Munster, scatter over the
cumin seeds and bake at 180°C (350°F/Gas 4) for 20 minutes.

158

COMTOISE PIE

SERVES 6
PREPARATION TIME 20 MINUTES, PLUS COOLING
TOTAL COOKING TIME 35 MINUTES

Serve hot, as an entrée or the cheese course

Traditional recipe from the Franche~Comté region

500 g (1 lb 2 oz) pâte feuilletée,
    or 2 packets puff pastry
200 g (7 oz) vieux (aged) Comté cheese
30 g (1 oz) butter
30 g (1 oz) plain (all-purpose) flour
100 ml (3½ fl oz) vin jaune or fino sherry
200 ml (7 fl oz) thin (pouring) cream
½ teaspoon ground nutmeg
Salt and pepper
6 slices Luxeuil ham, or other cooked ham
1 egg

EQUIPMENT
Round 20 cm (8 inch) cake tin

FILLING
Cut the Comté cheese into 1 cm (½ inch) cubes.
In a saucepan, melt the butter over medium heat and add the flour all at once, stirring constantly with a wooden spoon until the mixture comes away from the saucepan. Add the vin jaune, cream and nutmeg. Cook over low heat for 5 minutes, stirring constantly. Add the cheese, season lightly and allow to cool.

ASSEMBLY AND COOKING
Line the cake tin with baking paper, or grease and flour it. Roll out half the pastry dough until 3 mm (⅛ inch) thick and place it in the tin, allowing the edges to hang over the side by 1 cm (½ inch).
Pour in half the béchamel sauce, cover with the slices of ham and finish with the remaining béchamel.
Whisk the egg and use it to glaze the edges. Roll out the remaining pastry dough and cover the pie. Seal the two rounds of pastry dough together by pinching the edges. Glaze the top of the pie and bake at 180°C (350°F/Gas 4) for 30 minutes.

Cheese pies

MOZZARELLA IN A PISTACHIO CRUST

SERVES 6
PREPARATION TIME 20 MINUTES
TOTAL COOKING TIME 15 MINUTES

Serve hot, as an entrée or the cheese course

400 g (14 oz) pâte brisée,
    or 2 packets shortcrust (pie) pastry
3 balls fresh mozzarella, about 200 g (7 oz) each
45 ml (1½ fl oz) olive oil
3 teaspoons herbes de Provence
Fine sea salt
2 eggs
50 g (1¾ oz/⅓ cup) pistachios

MOZZARELLA FILLING
Drain the mozzarella and cut the balls in half. Brush them with the olive oil, sprinkle with the herbes de Provence and season with sea salt.

ASSEMBLY AND COOKING
Roll out the pastry dough until 3 mm (⅛ inch) thick. On a baking tray lined with baking paper, cut out six rounds about 12 cm (4½ inches) in diameter. Place a half ball of mozzarella on each round.
Whisk the eggs and use to glaze the edges. Bring the edges up around the mozzarella and close by pinching and twisting the dough lightly, like a money bag.
Glaze all over with egg, press the pistachios into the dough and bake at 180°C (350°F/Gas 4) for 15 minutes.

SWEET
PIES
with or without
FRUIT

CHERRY PIES

SERVES 6
PREPARATION TIME 25 MINUTES, PLUS COOLING
TOTAL COOKING TIME 30 MINUTES
RESTING TIME 20 MINUTES

Serve hot or cold, as a dessert

500 g (1 lb 2 oz) pâte sablée,
    or 2 packets sweet rich shortcrust pastry
500 g (1 lb 2 oz) ripe black cherries
200 g (7 oz) caster (superfine) sugar
2 tablespoons almond meal
30 ml (1 fl oz) kirsch
2 tablespoons medium-grain semolina
1 egg

EQUIPMENT
Six 9.5 cm (3¾ inch) pie tins with
    removable bases

CHERRY FILLING
Remove the stems of the cherries and pit them. Combine with the sugar, almond meal and kirsch.

ASSEMBLY AND COOKING
Lightly grease and flour the tins. Roll out half the pastry until 5 mm (¼ inch) thick and cut out 12 rounds.
Line the base and side of the tins with half the pastry rounds, then chill for 20 minutes. Place the lined tins on a baking tray, lined with baking paper and fill with dried beans or rice and bake at 180°C (350°F/Gas 4) for 10–15 minutes. Remove the paper and beans and cook for another 10 minutes or until golden and dry. Cool, then sprinkle the bases with semolina to absorb the excess juices. Fill with the cherry mixture. Whisk the egg and use it to glaze the edges. Cover the pies with the six remaining rounds and seal the edges together by pinching them. Decorate with the pastry offcuts and glaze with egg. Bake at 180°C (350°F/Gas 4) for 30 minutes.

LITTLE APPLE-CINNAMON PIES

SERVES 6
PREPARATION TIME 30 MINUTES, PLUS COOLING
TOTAL COOKING TIME 40 MINUTES
RESTING TIME 20 MINUTES

Serve hot or cold, as a dessert

500 g (1 lb 2 oz) pâte sablée,
   or 2 packets sweet rich shortcrust pastry
6 apples, such as granny smiths
50 g (1¾ oz) unsalted butter
100 g (3½ oz) caster (superfine) sugar
2 teaspoons ground cinnamon
1 egg

EQUIPMENT
Six 8 × 5.5 cm (3¼ × 2¼ inch) loaf (bar) tins

APPLE–CINNAMON FILLING
Peel the apples and cut them into 1 cm (½ inch) cubes.
Melt the butter in a frying pan over medium heat, add the
diced apples and sugar and cook for 5 minutes. Add the
cinnamon and cook for a further 5 minutes, then allow to cool.

ASSEMBLY AND COOKING
Grease and line the tins with baking paper. Roll out half of
the pastry dough until 5 mm (¼ inch) thick and cut out six
rectangles to line the base and sides of the tins, leaving
5 mm (¼ inch) overhanging. Set aside in the refrigerator
for 20 minutes. Once chilled, fill with the apple–cinnamon
mixture.
Whisk the egg and use it to glaze the edges. Roll out the
remaining dough, cut out six rectangles to cover the pies and
seal the edges together by pinching them. Decorate with the
pastry offcuts and glaze with egg. Bake at 180°C (350°F/
Gas 4) for 30 minutes.

APRICOT PIE

SERVES 6
PREPARATION TIME 20 MINUTES
TOTAL COOKING TIME 30 MINUTES

Serve this one cold, as a dessert

500 g (1 lb 2 oz) pâte feuilletée,
    or 2 packets puff pastry
500 g (1 lb 2 oz) fresh apricots
1 egg yolk
3 teaspoons honey
1 tablespoon pistachios
1 tablespoons sultanas
100 g (3½ oz) medium-grain semolina
100 g (3½ oz) blanched almonds
100 g (3½ oz) caster (superfine) sugar
3 teaspoons sesame seeds

EQUIPMENT
Round 20 cm (8 inch) cake tin

APRICOT FILLING
Pull the apricots apart into halves and remove the kernel.
Combine the egg yolk with the honey.

ASSEMBLY AND COOKING
Grease and flour the cake tin. Roll out two-thirds of the pastry
dough until 3 mm (⅛ inch) thick and place it in the tin, with
the edges hanging over the side.
Set aside some pistachios and sultanas. Sprinkle the base of
the pie with semolina to absorb the excess juices and arrange
the apricots, almonds, sugar and remaining pistachios and
sultanas on top.
Glaze the edges with the egg–honey mixture. Roll out the
remaining dough to make a second round and use it to cover
the pie. Seal the two rounds of pastry dough together by
pinching the edges. Glaze the top with the egg–honey mixture,
sprinkle with sesame seeds and scatter over the reserved nuts
and sultanas. Place on a pre-heated heavy-based baking tray
and bake at 180°C (350°F/Gas 4) for 30 minutes.

MAPLE SYRUP PIE

SERVES 8
PREPARATION TIME 20 MINUTES, PLUS COOLING
TOTAL COOKING TIME 40 MINUTES
RESTING TIME 20 MINUTES

Serve this one cold, as a dessert

500 g (1 lb 2 oz) pâte sablée,
      or 2 packets sweet rich shortcrust pastry
100 g (3½ oz) hazelnuts
100 g (3½ oz) slivered almonds
50 g (1¾ oz/⅓ cup) pistachios
50 g (1¾ oz/⅓ cup) pine nuts
100 g (3½ oz) raisins
150 g (5½ oz/⅔ cup) caster (superfine) sugar
60 ml (2 fl oz/¼ cup) maple syrup

EQUIPMENT
25 cm (10 inch) tart (flan) tin with removable base

TART BASE
Place the nuts on a baking tray and lightly toast at 180°C
(350°F/Gas 4) for 5 minutes, then rub the hazelnuts in a
clean tea towel (dish towel) to remove the skins.
Roll out two-thirds of the pastry dough until 3 mm (⅛ inch)
thick and place it in the tart tin. Refrigerate for 20 minutes.
Line the tart shell with baking paper then fill with dried beans
or rice, place on a baking tray and bake at 180°C (350°F/Gas 4)
for 15 minutes. Remove the paper and beans, then bake for
another 10 minutes or until the pastry is golden and dry.

MAPLE SYRUP AND NUT FILLING
Cook the sugar over low heat in a non-stick frying pan until
you have a pale caramel. Add the raisins, nuts and maple
syrup and mix well.

ASSEMBLY AND COOKING
Spread maple syrup and nut mixture over the tart base.
Cut out small circles from the remaining pastry dough,
place them on the filling, then bake at 180°C (350°F/Gas 4)
for 10 minutes.

APPLE FILO PARCEL

SERVES 6
PREPARATION TIME 30 MINUTES
TOTAL COOKING TIME 20 MINUTES

Serve hot, as a dessert

Traditional recipe from the South-West

8 sheets filo pastry
6 apples, such as royal galas
150 g (5½ oz) unsalted butter
200 g (7 oz) caster (superfine) sugar
100 g (3½ oz) flaked almonds
3 teaspoons cinnamon
200 ml (7 fl oz) Armagnac brandy

EQUIPMENT
20 cm (8 inch) spring-form cake tin

APPLE FILLING
Peel the apples and cut them into segments.
Melt 100 g (3½ oz) of butter in a non-stick frying pan, add
the apples and 150 g (5½ oz) of sugar and cook over low heat
for 15 minutes, turning the apples regularly. Add the flaked
almonds, cinnamon and 150 ml (5 fl oz) of the brandy.
Reduce until dry.

ASSEMBLY AND COOKING
Melt the remaining butter. Lay one sheet of filo pastry on the
work surface, brush with butter and sprinkle over a little of
the remaining sugar. Cover with a second sheet of pastry at a
45° angle to the first, and brush with butter and sprinkle with
sugar in the same way. Repeat the process, using all the sheets
of filo to form a rosette.
Arrange the layered filo sheets in a tin, so that the sheets
hang quite a way over the edges. Place the apple mixture
in the middle and fold in the corners of each of the sheets,
crumpling them at the same time. Bake at 180°C (350°F/
Gas 4) for 20 minutes.
Heat the remaining Armagnac in a saucepan, flambé and
pour over the pastry when serving.

CHOC-PEAR CRISP

**SERVES 6
PREPARATION TIME 25 MINUTES
TOTAL COOKING TIME 30 MINUTES**

Serve hot or cold, as a dessert

8 sheets filo pastry
4 firm pears
100 g (3½ oz) dark chocolate
100 g (3½ oz) milk chocolate
100 g (3½ oz) ground praline (caramelised almonds)
100 g (3½ oz) unsalted butter
100 g (3½ oz) icing (confectioners') sugar

CHOC-PEAR FILLING
Peel the pears and cut them into small 5 cm (2 inch) cubes. Chop the dark and milk chocolate and combine them with the diced pear and praline.

ASSEMBLY AND COOKING
Melt the butter. Lay out the sheets of filo pastry, brush with butter and sprinkle with 1 tablespoon of sugar.
Lay two sheets of filo on top of each other on a baking tray lined with baking paper. Top with one-third of the choc–pear mixture, leaving a 3 cm (1¼ inches) border on each short end, and cover with two more sheets of filo. Repeat this process until you have four layers of pastry.
Roll up widthways, tucking in the sides well. Brush with melted butter and sprinkle with the remaining sugar, then bake at 180°C (350°F/Gas 4) for 30 minutes.

POIRAT DU BERRY

SERVES 6
PREPARATION TIME 20 MINUTES
TOTAL COOKING TIME 20 MINUTES

Serve hot or cold, as a dessert

Traditional recipe from the Centre region

500 g (1 lb 2 oz) pâte sablée,
    or 2 packets sweet rich shortcrust pastry
4 williams pears
30 ml (1 fl oz) Cognac brandy
150 g (5½ oz/⅔ cup) caster (superfine) sugar
1½ tablespoons sour cream
1 egg

PEAR FILLING
Peel the pears, cut them in half and remove the core and seeds. Combine the cream, Cognac and 100 g (3½ oz) sugar.

ASSEMBLY AND COOKING
Divide the dough in half and roll out two rounds of the same size until about 5 mm (¼ inch) thick. Line a baking tray with baking paper and lay one round of pastry on top. Arrange the pear halves in a rosette pattern over the pastry base, leaving a 2 cm (¾ inch) border all around. Pour over the cream mixture. Whisk the egg and use it to glaze the edges. Cover with the second piece of pastry. Seal the two rounds of pastry dough together with the flat of a knife point to make a saw-tooth pattern. Brush the top with the egg and sprinkle with the remaining sugar. Bake at 180°C (350°F/Gas 4) for 20 minutes.

PRALINE PIE

SERVES 6
PREPARATION TIME 25 MINUTES
TOTAL COOKING TIME 30 MINUTES

Serve this one cold, as a dessert

500 g (1 lb 2 oz) pâte sablée,
     or 2 packets sweet rich shortcrust pastry
1 apple
1 pear
100 g (3½ oz) dried apricots
100 g (3½ oz) dried figs
1 teaspoon ground cinnamon
1½ tablespoons sour cream
200 g (7 oz) praline rouge (red candied almonds)
1 egg

EQUIPMENT
Round 20 cm (8 inch) cake tin

FRUIT–PRALINE FILLING
Peel the apple and pear and cut them into small 1 cm (½ inch) cubes. Do the same with the dried apricots and figs. Combine everything with the cinnamon and cream.
Process the praline in a food processor until coarsely chopped and set aside 1 tablespoon for decoration.

ASSEMBLY AND COOKING
Line the tin with baking paper, or grease and flour it. Roll out two-thirds of the pastry dough until 3 mm (⅛ inch) thick and place it in the tin, with the edges hanging over the side by 2 cm (¾ inch). Fill with the fruit–praline mixture.
Whisk the egg and use it to glaze the edges. Roll out the remaining dough to make a second round and use it to cover the pie. Seal the two rounds of pastry dough together by pinching the edges, glaze the top and scatter over the reserved chopped praline. Place on a pre-heated heavy-based baking tray and bake at 180°C (350°F/Gas 4) for 30 minutes.

GALETTE DES ROIS

SERVES 8
PREPARATION TIME 20 MINUTES
TOTAL COOKING TIME 45 MINUTES

Serve hot, as a dessert, a snack or at work!

375 g (13 oz) pâte feuilletée,
    or 2 packets puff pastry
180 g blanched almonds
180 g caster (superfine) sugar
180 g unsalted butter
4 eggs

EQUIPMENT
20 cm (8 inch) tart (flan) tin
Fève (pie charm)

FILLING
Process the almonds with the sugar in a food processor until finely chopped. Melt the butter, add it to the almond–sugar mixture, then incorporate 3 eggs. Set aside the yolk of the remaining egg.

ASSEMBLY AND COOKING
Line the tin with paper, or grease and flour it. Roll out two-thirds of the pastry dough until 3 mm (⅛ inch) thick and place it in the tin, allowing the edges to hang over the side by 1 cm (½ inch). Fill with the almond cream, not forgetting the *fève*!
Glaze the edges with the reserved egg yolk. Roll out the remaining pastry dough and cover the pie, pressing the edges to seal. Draw a rosette pattern on top using the tip of a knife. Place on a pre-heated heavy-based baking tray and bake at 180°C (350°F/Gas 4) for 45 minutes.

182

SWEET PINE NUT PIES

SERVES 6
PREPARATION TIME 30 MINUTES, PLUS COOLING
TOTAL COOKING TIME 35 MINUTES

Serve hot, as a dessert

250 g (9 oz) pâte sablée,
    or 1 packet rich sweet shortcrust pastry
50 g (1¾ oz/⅓ cup) pine nuts
50 g (1¾ oz/⅓ cup) hazelnuts
50 g (1¾ oz/⅓ cup) pistachios
1 orange
1 lemon
100 g (3½ oz) caster (superfine) sugar
60 g (2¼ oz/¼ cup) unsalted butter
3 teaspoons orange blossom water
50 g (1¾ oz) sultanas
50 g (1¾ oz) candied orange peel
1 egg

EQUIPMENT
Six 9.5 cm (3¾ inch) pie tins

FILLING
Place the nuts on a baking tray and lightly toast at 180°C (350°F/Gas 4) for 5 minutes, then rub the hazelnuts in a clean tea towel (dish towel) to remove the skins.
Zest and juice the orange and lemon.
In a frying pan, cook the sugar over low heat until you have a dark caramel. Pour in the juice and boil, stirring, for 30 seconds to deglaze the pan. Add the zests and the butter and cook for 5 minutes. Add the orange blossom water, sultanas, nuts and candied orange peel. Divide this mixture between six tins and allow to cool.

ASSEMBLY AND COOKING
Roll out the pastry dough until 3 mm (⅛ inch) thick and cut out six rounds a little larger than the pie tins.
Whisk the egg and use it to brush the edges of the tins. Cover with one round of pastry and brush again. Make a criss-cross pattern on the top with a knife and bake at 180°C (350°F/Gas 4) for 20 minutes.

AMERICAN PIES

SERVES 6
PREPARATION TIME 20 MINUTES
TOTAL COOKING TIME 30 MINUTES

Serve hot, as a dessert

Traditional recipe from the United States

500 g (1 lb 2 oz) pâte sablée,
    or 2 packets sweet rich shortcrust pastry
100 g (3½ oz) sultanas
45 ml (1½ fl oz) Armagnac brandy
600 g apples, such as reinette or golden delicious
100 g (3½ oz/½ cup, lightly packed) light
    brown sugar
1 lemon
1 teaspoon ground cinnamon
1½ tablespoons black cherry jam
1½ tablespoons crème fraîche
1 egg

EQUIPMENT
Six 200 ml (7 fl oz) pie tins with removable bases

APPLE FILLING

Combine the sultanas with the Armagnac and cover them with boiling water for 10 minutes.

Peel the apples, cut them into 1 cm (½ inch) cubes, then combine them with the sugar and the juice and zest of the lemon. Add the cinnamon, black cherry jam, crème fraîche and drained sultanas. Combine well, then pour into a sieve placed over a bowl. Reserve the liquid.

ASSEMBLY AND COOKING

Line the tins with baking paper, or grease and flour them.

Roll out two-thirds of the pastry dough until 3 mm (⅛ inch) thick and cut out six rounds. Place in the tins, allowing the edges to hang over the sides by 2 cm (¾ inch). Fill each tin with the apple–cherry mixture, then add 1 tablespoon of the reserved liquid to each pie.

Whisk the egg and use it to glaze the edges. Roll out the remaining dough and cut out six rounds to cover the pies. Seal each pie by pinching the edges together and trim around the edge of the tin.

Prick the top of the pies several times with the tip of a knife, place on a pre-heated heavy-based baking tray and bake at 180°C (350°F/Gas 4) for 30 minutes.

Tables & Index

What pastry
should I use for my pie?

189

What can I put in my pie?

What can I put in my pie?